London Local Authorities Act 2000

CHAPTER vii

ARRANGEMENT OF SECTIONS

51.   Defence of due diligence.
52.   Liability of directors, etc.

SCHEDULES:

ELIZABETH II

2000   CHAPTER vii

An Act to confer further powers upon local authorities in London; and for related purposes.   [20th July 2000]

WHEREAS—

(1) It is expedient that further and better provision should be made for the improvement and development of local government services in London and for the benefit of persons residing therein and that the powers of London borough councils and the common council of the City of London (hereinafter referred to as "London borough councils and the common council") should be extended and amended as provided in this Act:

(2) It is expedient that arrangements for the control of parking and the enforcement of parking restrictions in London should be amended and strengthened:

(3) It is expedient that London borough councils and the common council should have improved powers to control waste:

(4) It is expedient that the law relating to licensing should be amended in its application to London:

(5) It is expedient that London borough councils and the common council should have power to license and control busking:

(6) It is expedient that the other provisions contained in this Act should be enacted:

(7) The purposes of this Act cannot be effected without the authority of Parliament:

1972 c. 70.

(8) In relation to the promotion of the Bill for this Act the Westminster City Council have complied with the requirements of section 239 of the Local Government Act 1972 and the other participating councils (namely, the Common Council of the City of London and all the other London borough councils except for the council of the London borough of Barnet) have complied with the requirements of section 87 of the Local Government Act 1985:

1985 c. 51.

(9) In relation to the promotion of the Bill for this Act the London borough councils and the common council have acted through their representation in the Association of London Government, a non-statutory organisation whose membership consists of all the London borough councils and the common council:

May it therefore please Your Majesty that it may be enacted, and be it enacted, by the Queen's Most Excellent Majesty, by and with the advice and consent of the Lords Spiritual and Temporal, and Commons, in this present Parliament assembled, and by the authority of the same, as follows, that is to say:—

Part I

Preliminary

Citation and commencement.

1.—(1) This Act may be cited as the London Local Authorities Act 2000 and except where otherwise provided shall come into force at the end of the period of two months beginning with the date on which it is passed.

(2) The London Local Authorities Acts 1990 to 1996 and this Act may together be cited as the London Local Authorities Acts 1990 to 2000.

Interpretation.

2. In this Act, except as otherwise expressly provided or unless the context otherwise requires—

"authorised officer" means an officer of a participating council authorised by the council in writing to act in relation to the relevant provision of this Act;

"functions" includes powers and duties;

"participating council" means the common council in its capacity as a local authority and the council of any London borough other than Barnet; and "borough", "City" and "council" shall be construed accordingly.

Part II

Parking

Interpretation of Part II.
1984 c. 27.

1991 c. 40.

3.—(1) In this Part of this Act—

"the Act of 1984" means the Road Traffic Regulation Act 1984;

"the Act of 1991" means the Road Traffic Act 1991;

"designated parking place" means a parking place in the area of a participating council which is designated as a parking place under an order made under section 6, 9 or 45 of the Act of 1984;

"parking adjudicator" means a parking adjudicator appointed under section 73(3) of the Act of 1991;

"parking attendant" has the same meaning as in section 63A of the Act of 1984;

"special parking area" means a special parking area designated by an order made by the Secretary of State under section 76(1) of the Act of 1991.

(2) For the purposes of this Part of this Act, the owner of a vehicle shall be taken to be the person by whom the vehicle is kept.

(3) In determining, for the purposes of this Part of this Act, who was the owner of a vehicle at any time, it shall be presumed that the owner was the person in whose name the vehicle was at that time registered under the Vehicle Excise and Registration Act 1994.

4.—(1) This section does not apply to the council of the Royal Borough of Kensington and Chelsea.

(2) Where a participating council, on the basis of information provided by the use of a camera or any other device, has reason to believe that a penalty charge relating to a stationary vehicle in a designated parking place or a special parking area in the area of the council is payable under Part II of the Act of 1991 with respect to the vehicle, they may serve a penalty charge notice on the person appearing to them to be the owner of the vehicle.

(3) A participating council may not serve a penalty charge notice under this section after the expiry of the period of 28 days beginning with the date on which the penalty charge allegedly became payable.

(4) Subject to subsection (5) below, the Act of 1991 shall apply to a penalty charge notice served under this section as though it were a penalty charge notice issued under section 66(1) of that Act.

(5) In the application of the Act of 1991 to a penalty charge notice served under this section—

(*a*) for the reference to the parking attendant in section 66(3)(*a*) there shall be substituted a reference to the council;

(*b*) for the reference in paragraph 1(2)(*b*) of Schedule 6 to the parking attendant who issued the penalty charge notice there shall be substituted a reference to the council who served the penalty charge notice; and

(*c*) for the purpose of section 66(3)(*d*), the date of the notice shall be the date on which the penalty charge notice was served.

(6) A notice served under this section may be served in the same manner as a notice to owner under paragraph 10 of Schedule 6 to the Act of 1991.

5.—(1) Where a parking attendant attempts to issue a penalty charge notice in accordance with section 66(1) of the Act of 1991 but is prevented from doing so by any person, the council may serve a penalty charge notice on the person appearing to them to be the owner of the vehicle.

(2) A participating council may not serve a penalty charge notice under this section after the expiry of the period of 28 days beginning with the date on which the penalty charge allegedly became payable.

PART II
—*cont.*

1994 c. 22.

Service of penalty charge notice on the basis of information provided by camera, etc.

Service of penalty charge notice where parking attendant prevented from issuing a notice.

(3) Subject to subsection (4) below, the Act of 1991 shall apply to a penalty charge notice served under this section as though it were a penalty charge notice served under section 66(1) of that Act.

(4) In the application of the Act of 1991 to penalty charge notices served under this section—

(*a*) for the reference to the parking attendant in section 66(3)(*a*) there shall be substituted a reference to the council;

(*b*) for the reference in paragraph 1(2)(*b*) of Schedule 6 to the parking attendant who issued the penalty charge notice there shall be substituted a reference to the council who served the penalty charge notice;

(*c*) for the purpose of section 66(3)(*d*) as applied by this section, the date of the penalty charge notice shall be the date on which the penalty charge notice was served; and

(*d*) in paragraph 2(4) of Schedule 6, the following additional ground shall be inserted:—

"(g) that, in the case of a penalty charge notice served under section 5 of the London Local Authorities Act 2000, the parking attendant was not prevented from serving the penalty charge notice in accordance with section 66(1) of this Act.".

(5) A notice served under this section may be served in the same manner as a notice to owner under paragraph 10 of Schedule 6 to the Act of 1991.

Parking outside designated parking places.
1995 c. x.

6. In its application to participating councils, section 5 of the London Local Authorities Act 1995 shall have effect as follows:—

"Designated parking places.

5.—(1) There shall be a prohibition on the waiting of vehicles in the circumstances mentioned in subsection (2) below and such prohibition shall be enforceable as if it had been imposed by an order under section 6 of the Act of 1984.

(2) The circumstances in which the waiting of vehicles is prohibited under subsection (1) above are where—

(*a*) the vehicle is on the carriageway of a road and wholly or partly within a special parking area; and

(*b*) no part of the vehicle is within 50 centimetres of the edge of the carriageway; and

(*c*) the vehicle is not wholly within a designated parking place or any other part of a road in respect of which the waiting of vehicles is specifically authorised.

(3) Nothing in subsection (1) above shall require the placing of any traffic signs in connection with the prohibition thereby imposed.

(4) Nothing in this section shall prohibit the driver of a vehicle from causing it to stop in the circumstances mentioned in subsection (2) above—

(*a*) if the driver is prevented from proceeding by circumstances beyond his control or it is necessary for him to stop in order to avoid an accident;

(*b*) if the vehicle is stopped for the purpose of making a left or right turn;

(*c*) if the vehicle is being used for fire brigade, ambulance or police purposes;

(*d*) for so long as may be necessary up to a maximum of 20 minutes for the delivery or collection of goods or merchandise or the loading or unloading of the vehicle at any premises if that cannot reasonably be carried out as respects those premises without stopping in the circumstances mentioned in subsection (2) above;

(*e*) for so long as may be necessary to enable the vehicle, if it cannot be used for such purpose without stopping in the circumstances mentioned in subsection (2) above, to be used in connection with any building operation, demolition or excavation, the collection of waste by any participating council, the removal of any obstruction to traffic, the maintenance, improvement or reconstruction of the road, or the laying, erection, alteration, repair or cleaning of any traffic sign or sewer or of any main, pipe or apparatus for the supply of gas, water or electricity, or of any telegraph or telephone wires, cables, posts or supports;

(*f*) for so long as may be necessary for the purpose of enabling persons to board or alight from the vehicle.".

7.—(1) Subject to subsections (2) and (3) below, a participating council may not serve a notice to owner under paragraph 1(1) of Schedule 6 to the Act of 1991 (which makes provision, among other things, for the service of notices to owner in respect of unpaid penalty charges) or Schedule 1 to the London Local Authorities Act 1996 (which makes provision relating to the enforcement of the provisions in that Act relating to bus lanes) after the expiry of the period of six months from the date on which the relevant penalty charge notice was issued.

Limitation on service of notice to owner.

1996 c. ix.

(2) Subject to subsection (3) below, where—

(*a*) a notice to owner has been cancelled under paragraph 3 of the said Schedule 6; or

(*b*) a participating council has cancelled a notice to owner in compliance with a direction given by a parking adjudicator under paragraph 5(2) of the said Schedule 6; or

(*c*) a notice to owner is deemed to have been cancelled under paragraph 8(5)(*c*) of the said Schedule 6 (deemed cancellation where a statutory declaration under paragraph 8(2)(*a*) of that Schedule is served under paragraph 8(1)(*c*)),

the council may not serve a fresh notice to owner after the expiry of the period of six months from the date of the cancellation of the notice to owner or, in a case falling within paragraph (*c*) above, the date on which the council are served with notice under paragraph 8(5)(*d*) of the said Schedule 6.

(3) Where a council has before the expiry of 56 days from—

(*a*) the date on which the penalty charge notice was issued; or (*b*) the date of the cancellation of the notice to owner in the case where a notice to owner has been cancelled under paragraph 3 of the said Schedule 6 or in compliance with a direction given by a parking adjudicator under paragraph 5(2) of the said Schedule 6; or

(*c*) the date on which the council are served with notice under paragraph 8(5)(*d*) of the said Schedule 6 where the notice to owner is deemed to have been cancelled under paragraph 8(5)(*c*),

made a request to the Secretary of State for the supply of relevant particulars relating to the identity of the owner of the vehicle contained in the register of mechanically propelled vehicles maintained by him under

the Vehicle Excise and Registration Act 1994 and those particulars have not been supplied to the council before the date after which the council would not be entitled to serve a notice to owner or fresh notice to owner by virtue of subsection (1) or (2) above, the council shall continue to be entitled to serve a notice to owner or fresh notice to owner for a further period of 9 months beginning with that date.

8.—(1) Any charge certificate or notice under Schedule 6 to the Act of 1991 (which makes provision, among other things, in relation to parking penalties) or this Act may be served by a participating council by transmission by FAX or other means of electronic data transmission in accordance with subsections (2) and (3) below.

(2) A charge certificate or notice may be transmitted by FAX where the person on whom the charge certificate or notice is served has indicated in writing to the council that he is willing to regard a document as having been duly sent to him if it is transmitted to a specified FAX number and the document is transmitted to that number.

(3) Subsection (2) above shall apply with appropriate modification to a transmission of electronic data other than by FAX as it applies to a transmission by FAX.

(4) In this section, "FAX" means the making of a facsimile copy of a document by the transmission of electronic signals.

9. This section and sections 10 (Effect of removal or release) to 14 (Miscellaneous provisions relating to unpaid charges) of this Act shall apply in the area of a participating council where a vehicle has been removed by a parking attendant under section 99 of the Act of 1984 and regulations made thereunder or an immobilisation device has been fixed to a vehicle by a parking attendant or another person acting under his direction under section 69 or 77 of the Act of 1991 and the owner or person in charge of the vehicle lawfully removes it from the custody of the council or secures its release from the immobilisation device but does not, at the time the vehicle is so removed or released, pay any charges allegedly incurred of the kind mentioned in—

(*a*) section 101(4A)(*a*) or (*b*) of the Act of 1984; or

(*b*) section 69(4)(*a*) or (*b*) of the Act of 1991; or

(*c*) section 77(2) or (5) of the Act of 1991,

(hereinafter referred to as "charges allegedly incurred").

10.—(1) The removal or release of a vehicle in the circumstances mentioned in section 9 (Unpaid charges on release or removal of vehicle) of this Act shall not affect the liability of the owner or person in charge of the vehicle (hereinafter referred to as "the relevant person") to pay the charges allegedly incurred but when the relevant person removes the vehicle or secures its release he shall thereupon be informed of his right under section 11 (Representations relating to unpaid charges) of this Act to make representations to the council and of the effect of sections 12 (Appeals relating to unpaid charges) and 13 (Charge certificates relating to unpaid charges) of this Act.

(2) The participating council shall give that information, or shall cause it to be given, in writing.

11.—(1) The relevant person may make representations to the participating council on one or more of the following grounds:—

(*a*) that there were no reasonable grounds for the parking attendant concerned to believe that the vehicle had been permitted to remain at rest—

(i) in a designated parking place in circumstances specified in section 66(2)(*a*), (*b*) or (*c*) of the Act of 1991; or

(ii) in a special parking area (other than in a designated parking place) in circumstances in which an offence would have been committed in respect of the vehicle but for section 76(3) of the Act of 1991;

(*b*) that the vehicle had been permitted to remain at rest in the place in question by a person who was in control of the vehicle without the consent of the owner;

(*c*) that the place at which the vehicle was at rest was neither a designated parking place nor in a special parking area;

(*d*) in a case where the vehicle is released from an immobilisation device that, by virtue of an exemption given by section 70 of the Act of 1991, neither section 69 nor 77(4) of that Act applied to the vehicle at the time in question; or

(*e*) that the penalty or other charge in question exceeded the amount applicable in the circumstances of the case.

(2) A council may disregard any representations which are received by them after the end of the period of 28 days beginning with the date on which the person making them is informed, under subsection (1) of section 10 (Effect of removal or release) of this Act, of his right to make representations.

(3) It shall be the duty of a council to whom representations are duly made under this section, before the end of the period of 56 days beginning with the date on which they receive the representations—

(*a*) to consider them and any supporting evidence which the person making them provides; and

(*b*) to serve on that person notice of their decision as to whether they accept that the ground in question has been established.

(4) Where a participating council serve notice under subsection (3)(*b*) above that they accept that a ground has been established any charges

PART II —*cont.* Effect of removal or release.

Representations relating to unpaid charges.

allegedly incurred which were not paid at the time the vehicle was removed or released shall cease to be payable except to the extent (if any) to which those sums were properly payable and section 13 (Charge certificates relating to unpaid charges) of this Act shall not apply in relation to those charges except to the said extent.

(5) Where a participating council serve notice under subsection (3)(*b*) above that they do not accept that a ground has been established, that notice shall—

(*a*) inform the person on whom it is served of his right to appeal to a parking adjudicator under section 12 (Appeals relating to unpaid charges) of this Act;

(*b*) indicate the nature of a parking adjudicator's power to award costs against any person appealing to him under that section; and

(*c*) describe in general terms the form and manner in which such an appeal is required to be made.

(6) Where a participating council fail to comply with subsection (3) above before the end of the period of 56 days mentioned there—

(*a*) they shall be deemed to have accepted that the ground in question has been established and to have served notice to that effect under subsection (4) above; and

(*b*) immediately after the end of that period, subsection (4) above shall have effect in relation to any charges incurred in the manner set out in that subsection.

(7) A participating council may disregard any representations made under Schedule 6 to the Act of 1991 in respect of any charges allegedly incurred where representations are made in respect of those charges under this section.

Appeals relating to unpaid charges.

12.—(1) Where a participating council serve notice under subsection (3)(*b*) of section 11 (Representations relating to unpaid charges) of this Act that they do not accept that a ground on which representations were made under that subsection has been established, the person making those representations may, before—

(*a*) the end of the period of 28 days beginning with the date of service of that notice; or

(*b*) such longer period as a parking adjudicator may allow;

appeal to a parking adjudicator against the council's decision.

(2) On an appeal under this section, the parking adjudicator shall consider the representations in question and any additional representations which are made by the appellant on any of the grounds mentioned in subsection (1) of the said section 11 of this Act and, if he concludes that any of the representations are justified he shall direct that any charges which would have ceased to remain payable under subsections (4) or (6) of the said section 11 of this Act if the council had served notice that they accepted that the ground in question had been established shall so cease to remain payable and that section 13 (Charge certificates relating to unpaid charges) of this Act shall not apply in respect of those charges.

13.—(1) Where any charge allegedly incurred is not paid before the end of the relevant period, the participating council concerned may serve on the relevant person who removed it or secured its release a statement (hereinafter referred to as a "charge certificate") to the effect that any penalty charge in question is increased by 50 per cent and informing the person on whom the charge certificate is served of subsection (4) below.

PART II
— *cont.*

Charge certificates relating to unpaid charges.

(2) The relevant period is the period of 28 days beginning—

(*a*) where no representations are made under subsection (1) of section 11 (Representations relating to unpaid charges) of this Act, with the date on which the vehicle is released or removed from the custody of the council concerned;

(*b*) where—

(i) such representations are made;

(ii) the council serve notice under subsection (3)(*b*) of the said section 11 of this Act that they do not accept that a ground has been established (hereinafter referred to as "a notice of rejection"); and

(iii) no appeal against the notice of rejection is made under section 12 (Appeals relating to unpaid charges) of this Act with the date on which the notice of rejection is served; or

(*c*) where there has been an unsuccessful appeal against a notice of rejection, with the date on which notice of the adjudicator's decision is served on the appellant.

(3) Where an appeal against a notice of rejection is made but is withdrawn before the adjudicator gives notice of his decision, the relevant period is the period of 14 days beginning with the date on which the appeal is withdrawn.

(4) Where a charge certificate has been served on any person and any increased penalty charge or any other charge provided for in the certificate is not paid before the end of the period of 14 days beginning with the date on which the certificate is served, the council concerned may, if a county court so orders, recover the increased penalty charge or other charge as if it were payable under a county court order.

(5) Subject to section 8 (Service of notices) of this Act, any charge certificate under this section—

(*a*) may be served by post; and

(*b*) where the person on whom it is to be served is a body corporate, is duly served if it is sent by post to the secretary or clerk of that body.

14.—(1) Schedule 6 to the Act of 1991 (which provides, among other things, for parking penalties) shall not apply in relation to penalty charge notices issued in any case where the provisions of this section apply.

Miscellaneous provisions relating to unpaid charges.

(2)(*a*) A person who makes any representation under section 11 (Representations relating to unpaid charges) or section 12 (Appeals relating to unpaid charges) of this Act which is false in a material particular and does so recklessly or knowing it to be false in that particular is guilty of an offence.

(*b*) Any person convicted of an offence under this subsection shall be liable on summary conviction to a fine not exceeding level 5 on the standard scale.

(3) (*a*) Any notice required to be served under this subsection may be served by post.

(*b*) Where the person on whom any document is required to be served by subsection (3) of the said section 11 of this Act is a body corporate, the document is duly served if it is sent by post to the secretary or clerk of that body.

Parking on footways, grass verges, etc.
1974 c. xxiv.

15.—(1) Section 15 of the Greater London Council (General Powers) Act 1974 (As to parking on footways, grass verges, etc.) shall apply in the area of a participating council in accordance with the following subsections.

(2) Subsection (1) is replaced by the following subsection:—

"(1) Save as provided in subsections (3), (4), (7) and (11), any person who causes or permits any vehicle to be parked in Greater London with one or more wheels on any part of an urban road other than a carriageway, shall be guilty of an offence and shall be liable on summary conviction to a fine not exceeding level 1 on the standard scale.".

(3) In subsection (3) in paragraph (*d*), after the word "goods" the words "for a period not exceeding 20 minutes or such longer period as the council may permit" are inserted.

(4) In subsection (4)—

(*a*) the words "any such footway, grass verge, garden, space or land as is referred to in subsection (1) of this section and is in or on any highway" are replaced by the words "any part of an urban road which is a highway other than a carriageway"; and

(*b*) the words "footway, grass verge, garden, space or land" are replaced by the words "urban road".

(5) In subsection (5) the words "footway, grass verge, garden, space or land" are replaced by the words "urban road".

(6) In subsection (7) at the end of paragraph (*b*) the following paragraph is inserted—

"(*c*) The highway authority may charge such fees for the specification of vehicles under sub-paragraph (xii) of the foregoing paragraph as they may determine and as may be sufficient in the aggregate to cover in whole or in part the reasonable administrative or other costs in connection with their functions under that sub-paragraph.".

Powers of entry.

16.—(1) This section applies where a vehicle has been removed from a road in the area of a participating council by a parking attendant under section 99 of the Act of 1984 and regulations made thereunder.

(2) An authorised officer may, at any time after the removal of the vehicle and before the vehicle is lawfully removed from the custody of the council or is disposed of under section 101 of the Act of 1984, enter the vehicle for the purpose of removing anything in it in the interests of the

safety of persons or property outside the vehicle or for the prevention of damage to or loss of the vehicle or any of its contents.

(3) Subject to subsection (4) below, a council shall retain and keep safe anything removed under subsection (2) above and shall deliver it to any person claiming it who satisfies the council that he is the owner of it or of the vehicle in question.

(4) Where the vehicle from which anything is removed under subsection (2) above is disposed of under section 101(1) of the Act of 1984 the council may also, in any manner they think fit, dispose of the thing removed if it has not been claimed by any person who satisfies the council that he is its owner.

PART III

PUBLIC HEALTH

17.—(1) In this Part of this Act—

"the Act of 1936" means the Public Health Act 1936;

"the Act of 1990" means the Environmental Protection Act 1990;

"cleansing notice" means a notice served under subsection (1) of section 19 (Cleansing relevant land of litter and refuse) of this Act;

"relevant land" means any street in the area of a participating council together with any land which is in the open air and is adjacent to such a street otherwise than land comprised in a highway but does not include—

(*a*) any land which a person has a duty to ensure is, so far as is practicable, kept clear of litter and refuse by virtue of section 89 of the Act of 1990; or

(*b*) any canal or inland navigation belonging to or under the control of the British Waterways Board, or any works, lands or premises belonging to or under the control of the British Waterways Board and held or used by them in connection with such canal or inland navigation;

"relevant premises" means—

(*a*) premises which front or abut on relevant land; and

(*b*) premises which are served by the relevant land as a means of access; and

(*c*) where any such premises as are mentioned in paragraph (*a*) above form part of a building in which other premises are situated, those other premises;

"street" has the same meaning as in section 343 (Interpretation) of the Act of 1936 but does not include a highway;

"waste control enactments" means—

(*a*) the following sections of the Act of 1990:—

(i) section 45 (Collection of controlled waste); and

(ii) section 46 (Receptacles for household waste); and

(iii) section 47 (Receptacles for commercial or industrial waste); and

Interpretation of Part III.
1936 c. 49.

1990 c. 43.

(*b*) section 19 (Cleansing relevant land of litter and refuse) of this Act.

(2) The definitions in section 75 of the Act of 1990 shall apply for the purposes of this Part of this Act.

**Enforcement of waste control enactments.
1974 c. 40.**

18. The following sections of the Control of Pollution Act 1974 shall have effect as if references therein to that Act included references to the waste control enactments—

(*a*) section 91 (Rights of entry and inspection, etc.); and

(*b*) section 92 (Provisions supplementary to s. 91).

Cleansing relevant land of litter and refuse.

19.—(1) A participating council may by notice specify the standards and frequency at which relevant land requires to be swept and cleansed so as to keep it reasonably clear of litter and refuse and shall serve a copy of such notice on the owner of the relevant land or the owner or occupier of any relevant premises.

(2) If, at any time after the expiration of 42 days from the service of the cleansing notice, the council determine that the relevant land is not being swept and cleansed in accordance with the notice then the council shall give notice of this determination to the person on whom the cleansing notice was served and may cause the relevant land to be swept and cleansed.

(3) At any time the council may decide to revoke any cleansing notice or any determination made under subsection (2) above and shall give notice of any such decision to the person who was served with the cleansing notice or the determination, as the case may be and may serve a fresh cleansing notice or make a fresh determination as the case may be.

(4) A person served with a cleansing notice or a notice under subsection (2) above may appeal to a magistrates' court acting for the petty sessions area in which the relevant land is situated on any of the following grounds which are appropriate in the circumstances of the particular case:—

(*a*) that the notice or requirement under the notice is not justified by the terms of this section;

(*b*) that there has been some informality, defect or error in, or in connection with, the notice;

(*c*) that the standards and frequency at which the sweeping and cleansing is to be carried out are unreasonable;

(*d*) that it would have been equitable for the notice to have been served on the occupier of the premises in question instead of on the owner, or on the owner instead of on the occupier;

(*e*) where the sweeping and cleansing is for the common benefit of the premises in question and other premises, that some other person, being the owner or occupier of premises to be benefited, ought to contribute towards the expenses of executing any works required.

(5) If and in so far as an appeal under this section is based on the ground of some informality, defect or error in or in connection with the notice, the court shall dismiss the appeal, if it is satisfied that the informality, defect or error was not a material one.

(6) Where the grounds upon which an appeal under this section is brought include a ground specified in paragraph (*d*) or paragraph (*e*) of subsection (4) above, the appellant shall serve a copy of his notice of appeal on each other person referred to, and in the case of any appeal under this section may serve a copy of his notice of appeal on any other person having an estate or interest in the premises in question, and on the hearing of the appeal the court may make such order as it thinks fit with respect to the person by whom any sweeping and cleansing is to be carried out and the contribution to be made by any other person towards the cost of the work, or as to the proportions in which any expenses which may become recoverable by the council are to be borne by the appellant and such other person.

In exercising its powers under this subsection, the court shall have regard—

    (*a*) as between an owner and an occupier, to the terms and conditions whether contractual or statutory, of the tenancy and to the nature of the works required; and

    (*b*) in any case, to the degree of benefit to be derived by the different persons concerned.

(7) Subject to such right of appeal as aforesaid, where the council causes land to be swept and cleansed under subsection (2) above, they may recover from the person on whom the cleansing notice was served the expenses reasonably incurred by them in so doing.

(8) In proceedings by the council for the recovery of any expenses under subsection (7) above, it shall not be open to the defendant to raise any question which he could have raised on an appeal under this section.

(9) Sections 275, 283(1), 285, 289 and 300 of the Act of 1936 shall apply to a cleansing notice.

(10) Sections 278, 283(1), 285, 291 and 300 of the Act of 1936 shall apply to a notice under subsection (2) above.

(11) The sections of the Act of 1936 mentioned in subsections (9) and (10) above shall apply to notices served under this section as if—

    (*a*) references therein to that Act included references to this section; and

    (*b*) references therein to the execution of works included references to the carrying out of sweeping and cleansing and cognate terms shall be construed accordingly.

(12) Section 291 of the Act of 1936 shall apply to notices served under subsection (2) above as if references to the owner of the premises in respect of which the expenses were incurred included references to the person on whom the cleansing notice was served.

20. Where a cleansing notice is served in respect of relevant land—

    (*a*) if the land is swept and cleansed in accordance with the notice any resulting litter or refuse left for removal shall be treated as commercial waste; and

    (*b*) if the land is swept and cleansed by the council in pursuance of subsection (2) of section 19 (Cleansing relevant land of litter and refuse) of this Act any such litter or refuse shall be treated as household waste.

PART III
—cont.
Offence of
leaving litter.

21. Section 87 of the Act of 1990 (which provides for an offence of leaving litter) shall apply to any relevant land in respect of which a cleansing notice has been served in so far as that land does not constitute a public open place for the purposes of the said section 87.

PART IV

LICENSING

Music and
dancing, sports,
boxing and
wrestling
licences.
1963 c. 33.

22.—(1) Schedule 12 to the London Government Act 1963 is amended in accordance with the following subsections in its application to the area of a participating council and that schedule, as amended by this Act is set out in Schedule 1 to this Act.

(2) In paragraph 1—

    (*a*) in sub-paragraph (1) the words "Subject to sub-paragraph (6) of this paragraph" are left out;

    (*b*) in sub-paragraph (2)—

        (i) the words "any applicant therefor" are replaced by the words "an applicant";

        (ii) after the word "renew" the words "or transfer" are inserted;

    (*c*) sub-paragraph (5) is left out;

    (*d*) in sub-paragraph (6) the words "the Theatre Royal Drury Lane, the Royal Covent Garden Opera House, the Theatre Royal Haymarket or to" are left out.

(3) In paragraph 3A—

    (*a*) in sub-paragraph (4)—

        (i) the words "any applicant" are replaced by the words "an applicant";

        (ii) after the word "renew" the words "or transfer" are inserted;

    (*b*) sub-paragraph (7) is left out.

(4) In paragraph 4—

    (*a*) in sub-paragraph (3)—

        (i) the words "any applicant therefor" are replaced by the words "an applicant";

        (ii) after the word "renew" the words "or transfer" are inserted; and

    (*b*) sub-paragraph (6) is left out.

(5) In paragraph 6A, at the beginning, the words "Subject to paragraph 6C of this Schedule," are inserted.

(6) In paragraph 6B, at the beginning, the words "Subject to paragraph 6C of this Schedule," are inserted.

PART IV
—cont.

(7) At the end of paragraph 6B, the following paragraphs are inserted:—

"6C.—(1) The following provisions of this paragraph shall have effect as respects cases where, before the date of expiry of a licence granted under paragraph 1, 3A or 4 of this Schedule an application for renewal of the licence has been made ("a renewal case") or an application for transfer of the licence has been made ("a transfer case").

(2) If the application is not determined before the prospective expiry date, the licence shall not be deemed to remain in force under paragraph 6A or 6B of this Schedule, as the case may be, after that date and the application shall be deemed to be withdrawn on that date, unless before then the applicant pays the council a continuation fee.

(3) Where a continuation fee is paid in pursuance of sub-paragraph (2) of this paragraph in a renewal case, the applicant's application for renewal shall be deemed to be an application for renewal for a period of twelve months starting on the day following the prospective expiry date.

(4) Where a continuation fee is paid in pursuance of sub-paragraph (2) of this paragraph in a transfer case—

(a) the applicant shall be deemed to have made an application for the renewal of the licence for a period of twelve months starting on the day following the prospective expiry date;

(b) the Council shall determine the application for transfer and deemed application for renewal together; and

(c) in the following provisions of this paragraph, references to "the application" in a transfer case are references to the application for transfer and the application for renewal.

(5) If the application is not determined before the date of the expiry of the renewal period under sub-paragraph (3) or (4) of this paragraph, as the case may be, the licence shall not be deemed to remain in force under paragraph 6A or 6B of this Schedule, as the case may be, after that date, and the application shall be deemed to be withdrawn on that date, unless before then the applicant pays the council a further continuation fee.

(6) Where a further continuation fee is paid in pursuance of sub-paragraph (5) of this paragraph, then—

(a) in a renewal case, the applicant's application for renewal shall be deemed to be an application for renewal for a period starting on the day following the date of the expiry of the renewal period under sub-paragraph (3) of this paragraph; and

(b) in a transfer case, the applicant's application so far as it is a deemed application for renewal shall be deemed to be an application for renewal for a period starting on the day following the date of the expiry of the renewal period under sub-paragraph (4) of this paragraph.

(7) A deemed application for renewal under paragraph (6) shall be for a period expiring—

    (*a*) where the application is withdrawn, on the date of withdrawal;

    (*b*) where the application is refused, on the date of the refusal;

    (*c*) where the application is granted, on one or other of the following:—

        (i) the date twelve months after the beginning of the period; or

        (ii) such other date as may be specified by the Council when allowing the application.

(8) In this paragraph—

"the prospective expiry date" means—

    (*a*) in a transfer case, the date on which the licence would have expired if the application for transfer had not been made; and

    (*b*) in a renewal case, the date of the expiry of the period in respect of which the application for renewal of the licence was made;

"a continuation fee" is a fee of the same amount as the fee payable in respect of an application for renewal of a licence.

6D. Where an applicant for the transfer of a licence granted under paragraph 1, 3A or 4 of this Schedule is carrying on at the premises in respect of which the licence was granted the functions to which the licence relates, "any necessary modifications" where those words appear in paragraph 6B of this Schedule, means the substitution for the name of the licence holder of the name of the applicant for the transfer of the licence and any other necessary modifications.".

(8) Paragraph 9 is left out and the following paragraph is inserted:—

"9.—(1) The Council may make regulations prescribing standard conditions applicable to all, or any class of, licences which may be granted under paragraph 1, 3A or 4 of this Schedule.

(2) Where the Council have made regulations under this paragraph, every licence granted, renewed or transferred by them shall be deemed to have been so granted, renewed or transferred subject to any standard conditions except so far as they are expressly excluded or amended in any particular case.".

(9) In paragraph (2) of paragraph 10 at the end of sub-paragraph (a) the following sub-paragraph is inserted:—

"(*aa*) any person is an applicant for the transfer of a licence granted under paragraph 1, 3A or 4 of this Schedule where he is carrying on at the premises in respect of which the licence was granted the functions to which the licence relates in respect of any premises which have been used in contravention of any term, condition or restriction on or subject to which the licence is held; or".

(10) In paragraph 17—

    (*a*) In sub-paragraph (1) the words "in accordance with plans deposited" are left out; and (*b*) In sub-paragraph (2)—

(i) the words ", on an application being made for the appropriate variation of the licence," are inserted after the word "shall";

(ii) the words "plans aforesaid" are replaced by the words "requirements aforesaid"; and

(iii) the words "plans as modified with the approval of the Council" are replaced with the words "requirements as modified by the Council".

(11) In paragraph 19—

(*a*) at the beginning of sub-paragraph (3) the words "Subject to paragraph 19AA of this Schedule" are inserted; and

(*b*) at the end of sub-paragraph (4) the following sub-paragraph is added:—

"(5) Where any licence is renewed under paragraph 1, 3A or 4 of this Schedule and the Council specify any term, condition or restriction which was not previously specified in relation to that licence, the licence shall be deemed to be free of it until the time for bringing an appeal under this paragraph has expired and, if such an appeal is duly brought, until the determination or abandonment of the appeal.".

(12) Before paragraph 19A, the following paragraph is inserted:—

"19AA.—(1) The following provisions of this paragraph shall have effect as respects cases where an appeal under paragraph 19 of this Schedule is brought, within the period for doing so, against the revocation of a licence ("a revocation case") or against the refusal of an application for renewal of a licence ("a refusal case").

(2) If the appeal is not determined before the prospective expiry date, the licence shall not be deemed to remain in force under paragraph 19(3) of this Schedule after that date, and the appeal shall be deemed to be abandoned on that date, unless before then—

(*a*) in a revocation case, the appellant makes an application for the renewal of the licence for a period of twelve months starting on the day following the prospective expiry date;

(*b*) in a refusal case the appellant pays the council a continuation fee.

(3) Where a continuation fee is paid in pursuance of sub-paragraph (2)(*b*) of this paragraph, the appellant's refused application for renewal shall be deemed to be an application for renewal for a period of twelve months starting on the day following the prospective expiry date.

(4) If the appeal is not determined before the date of the expiry of the renewal period under sub-paragraph (2)(*a*) or (3) of this paragraph, as the case may be, the licence shall not be deemed to remain in force under paragraph 19(3) of this Schedule after that date, and the appeal shall be deemed to be abandoned on that date,

unless before then the appellant pays the council a continuation fee or, as the case may be, a further continuation fee.

(5) Where a continuation fee or a further continuation fee is paid in pursuance of sub-paragraph (4) of this paragraph, the appellant's application for renewal or, as the case may be, refused application for renewal shall be deemed to be an application for renewal for a period starting on the day following the date of the expiry of the renewal period under sub-paragraph (2)(*a*) or, as the case may be, sub-paragraph (3) of this paragraph.

(6) A deemed application for renewal under sub-paragraph (5) shall be for a period expiring—

(*a*) where the appeal is withdrawn, on the date of withdrawal;

(*b*) where the appeal is unsuccessful—

(i) if a further appeal is available but is not made within the period for doing so, on the date of the expiry of that period;

(ii) if no further appeal is available, on the date of the decision of the court;

(*c*) where the appeal is successful, on the day before the date of the next anniversary of the beginning of the period; provided that where the period, at the time of the decision of the court, has been running for more than twelve months, the court may specify an earlier date.

(7) In this paragraph—

"the prospective expiry date" means—

(*a*) in a revocation case, the date on which the licence would have expired if it had not been revoked; and

(*b*) in a refusal case, the date of the expiry of the period in respect of which the refused application for renewal of the licence was made;

"a continuation fee" is a fee of the same amount as the fee payable in respect of an application for renewal of a licence.".

Private places of entertainment.
1967 c. 19.

23.—(1) The Private Places of Entertainment (Licensing) Act 1967 applies to the area of a participating council in accordance with the following subsections.

(2) In section 3—

(*a*) in subsection (1) after the word "renew" the words "or transfer" are inserted; and

(*b*) subsection (3) is left out.

(3) The following sections are inserted after section 3A:—

"Renewal and transfer of licence.

3B.—(1) Subject to section 3C of this Act, where, before the date of expiry of a licence granted under this Act, an application has been made for the renewal of that licence, the licence shall be deemed to remain in force, notwithstanding that the date of expiry of the licence has passed, until the determination of the application by the licensing authority or the withdrawal of the application.

(2) Subject to section 3C of this Act, where, before the date of expiry of a licence granted under this Act, an application has been made for the transfer of that licence, the licence shall be deemed to remain in force with any necessary modifications notwithstanding that the date of expiry of the licence has passed, until the determination of the application by the licensing authority or the withdrawal of the application.

(3) Where an applicant for the transfer of a licence granted under this Act is carrying on at the premises in respect of which the licence was granted the functions to which the licence relates, "any necessary modifications" where those words appear in subsection (2) of this section, means the substitution for the name of the licence holder of the name of the applicant for the transfer of the licence and any other necessary modifications.

Renewal and transfer of licence: supplementary.

3C.—(1) The following provisions of this section shall have effect as respects cases where, before the date of expiry of a licence granted under this Act, an application for renewal of the licence has been made ("a renewal case") or an application for transfer of the licence has been made ("a transfer case").

(2) If the application is not determined before the prospective expiry date, the licence shall not be deemed to remain in force under section 3B(1) or section 3B(2) of this Act, after that date and the application shall be deemed to be withdrawn on that date, unless before then the applicant pays the council a continuation fee.

(3) Where a continuation fee is paid in pursuance of subsection (2) of this section in a renewal case, the applicant's application for renewal shall be deemed to be an application for renewal for a period of twelve months starting on the day following the prospective expiry date.

(4) Where a continuation fee is paid in pursuance of subsection (2) of this section in a transfer case—

(a) the applicant shall be deemed to have made an application for the renewal of the licence for a period of twelve months starting on the day following the prospective expiry date;

(b) the Council shall determine the application for transfer and deemed application for renewal together; and

(c) in the following provisions of this section, references to "the application" in a transfer case are references to the application for transfer and the application for renewal.

(5) If the application is not determined before the date of the expiry of the renewal period under subsection (3) or (4) of this section, as the case may be, the licence shall not be deemed to remain in force under section 3B(1) or 3B(2) of this section, as the case may be, after that date, and the application shall be deemed to be withdrawn on that date, unless before then the applicant pays the council a further continuation fee.

(6) Where a further continuation fee is paid in pursuance of subsection (5) of this section, then—

(*a*) in a renewal case, the applicant's application for renewal shall be deemed to be an application for renewal for a period starting on the day following the date of the expiry of the renewal period under subsection (3) of this section; and

(*b*) in a transfer case, the applicant's application so far as it is a deemed application for renewal shall be deemed to be an application for renewal for a period starting on the day following the date of the expiry of the renewal period under subsection (4) of this section.

(7) A deemed application for renewal under subsection (6) shall be for a period expiring—

(*a*) where the application is withdrawn, on the date of withdrawal;

(*b*) where the application is refused, on the date of the refusal;

(*c*) where the application is granted, on one or other of the following:—

(i) the date twelve months after the beginning of the period; or

(ii) such other date as may be specified by the Council when allowing the application.

(8) In this section—

"the prospective expiry date" means—

(*a*) in a transfer case, the date on which the licence would have expired if the application for transfer had not been made; and

(*b*) in a renewal case, the date of the expiry of the period in respect of which the application for renewal of the licence was made;

"a continuation fee" is a fee of the same amount as the fee payable in respect of an application for renewal of a licence.

Provisional grant of licences.

3D.—(1) Where application is made to the licensing authority for the grant of a licence under this Act in respect of premises which are to be, or are in the course of being, constructed, extended or altered and the licensing authority are satisfied that the premises would, if completed in accordance with the requirements of the licensing authority, be such that the licensing authority would grant the licence, the licensing authority may grant the licence subject to a condition that it shall be of no effect until confirmed by the licensing authority.

(2) The licensing authority shall, on application being made for the appropriate variation of the licence, confirm any licence granted by virtue of the foregoing subsection if and when they are satisfied that the premises have been completed in accordance with the requirements aforesaid, or in accordance with those requirements as modified by the licensing authority, and that the licence is held by a fit and proper person.

Power to prescribe standard terms, conditions and restrictions.

3E.—(1) The licensing authority may make regulations prescribing standard conditions applicable to all, or any class of licences which may be granted under this Act.

(2) Where the licensing authority have made regulations under this section, every licence granted, renewed or transferred by them shall be deemed to have been so granted, renewed or transferred subject to any standard conditions applicable to it except so far as they are expressly excluded or amended in any particular case.".

(4) In subsection (2) of section 4—

(*a*) "(i)" is inserted after "(*a*)"; and

(*b*) the word "and" where it appears at the end of paragraph (*a*) is replaced by the words—"; or

(ii) an applicant for the transfer of the licence where he is carrying on the functions to which the licence relates; and".

(5) In section 5, at the beginning of subsection (5) the words "Subject to section 5B below" are inserted.

(6) After section 5A, the following section is inserted:—

"Appeals: supplementary provisions.

5B.—(1) The following provisions of this section shall have effect as respects cases where an appeal under section 5 of this Act is brought, within the period for doing so, against the revocation of a licence ("a revocation case") or against the refusal of an application for renewal of a licence ("a refusal case").

(2) If the appeal is not determined before the prospective expiry date, the licence shall not be deemed to remain in force under section 5(5) of this Act after that date, and the appeal shall be deemed to be abandoned on that date, unless before then—

(*a*) in a revocation case, the appellant makes an application for the renewal of the licence for a period of twelve months starting on the day following the prospective expiry date;

(*b*) in a refusal case the appellant pays the council a continuation fee.

(3) Where a continuation fee is paid in pursuance of subsection (2)(*b*) of this section, the appellant's refused application for renewal shall be deemed to be an application for renewal for a period of twelve months starting on the day following the prospective expiry date.

(4) If the appeal is not determined before the date of the expiry of the renewal period under subsection (2)(*a*) or (3) of this section, as the case may be, the licence shall not be deemed to remain in force under section 5(5) of this Act after that date, and the appeal shall be deemed to be abandoned on that date, unless before then the appellant pays the council a continuation fee or, as the case may be, a further continuation fee.

(5) Where a continuation fee or a further continuation fee is paid in pursuance of subsection (4) above, the appellant's application for renewal or, as the case may be, refused application for renewal shall be deemed to be an application for renewal for a period starting on the day following the date of the expiry of the

PART IV
—*cont.*

renewal period under subsection (2)(*a*) above or, as the case may be, subsection (3) above.

(6) A deemed application for renewal under subsection (5) shall be for a period expiring—

(*a*) where the appeal is withdrawn, on the date of withdrawal;

(*b*) where the appeal is unsuccessful—

(i) if a further appeal is available but is not made within the period for doing so, on the date of the expiry of that period;

(ii) if no further appeal is available, on the date of the decision of the court;

(*c*) where the appeal is successful, on the day before the date of the next anniversary of the beginning of the period; provided that where the period, at the time of the decision of the court, has been running for more than twelve months, the court may specify an earlier date.

(7) In this section—

"the prospective expiry date" means—

(*a*) in a revocation case, the date on which the licence would have expired if it had not been revoked; and

(*b*) in a refusal case, the date of the expiry of the period in respect of which the refused application for renewal of the licence was made;

"a continuation fee" is a fee of the same amount as the fee payable in respect of an application for renewal of a licence.".

Theatres.
1968 c. 54.

24.—(1) The Theatres Act 1968 applies to the area of a participating council in accordance with the following subsections.

(2) In subsection (2) of section 13—

(*a*) "(i)" is inserted after "(*a*)"; and

(*b*) the word "and" where it appears at the end of paragraph (*a*) is replaced by the words—"; or

(ii) an applicant for the transfer of the licence where he is carrying on the functions to which the licence relates; and".

(3) In section 14 at the beginning of subsection (3) the words "Subject to section 14A below" are inserted.

(4) After section 14, the following section is inserted:—

"Appeals: supplementary provisions.

14A.—(1) The following provisions of this section shall have effect as respects cases where an appeal under section 14 of this Act is brought, within the period for doing so, against the revocation of a licence ("a revocation case") or against the refusal of an application for renewal of a licence ("a refusal case").

(2) If the appeal is not determined before the prospective expiry date, the licence shall not be deemed to remain in force under section 14(3) of this Act after that date, and the appeal shall be deemed to be abandoned on that date, unless before then—

(*a*) in a revocation case, the appellant makes an application for the renewal of the licence for a period of twelve months starting on the day following the prospective expiry date;

(*b*) in a refusal case the appellant pays the council a continuation fee.

(3) Where a continuation fee is paid in pursuance of subsection (2)(*b*) above, the appellant's refused application for renewal shall be deemed to be an application for renewal for a period of twelve months starting on the day following the prospective expiry date.

(4) If the appeal is not determined before the date of the expiry of the renewal period under subsection (2)(*a*) or (3) above, as the case may be, the licence shall not be deemed to remain in force under section 14(3) of this Act after that date, and the appeal shall be deemed to be abandoned on that date, unless before then the appellant pays the council a continuation fee or, as the case may be, a further continuation fee.

(5) Where a continuation fee or a further continuation fee is paid in pursuance of subsection (4) above, the appellant's application for renewal or, as the case may be, refused application for renewal shall be deemed to be an application for renewal for a period starting on the day following the date of the expiry of the renewal period under subsection (2)(*a*) above or, as the case may be, subsection (3) above.

(6) A deemed application for renewal under subsection (5) shall be for a period expiring—

(*a*) where the appeal is withdrawn, on the date of withdrawal;

(*b*) where the appeal is unsuccessful—

(i) if a further appeal is available but is not made within the period for doing so, on the date of the expiry of that period;

(ii) if no further appeal is available, on the date of the decision of the court;

(*c*) where the appeal is successful, on the day before the date of the next anniversary of the beginning of the period; provided that where the period, at the time of the decision of the court, has been running for more than twelve months, the court may specify an earlier date.

(7) In this section—

"the prospective expiry date" means—

(*a*) in a revocation case, the date on which the licence would have expired if it had not been revoked; and

(*b*) in a refusal case, the date of the expiry of the period in respect of which the refused application for renewal of the licence was made;

"a continuation fee" is a fee of the same amount as the fee payable in respect of an application for renewal of a licence.".

(5) In Schedule 1—

(*a*) in sub-paragraph 1(1), after the word "renew" the words "or transfer" are inserted;

(*b*) sub-paragraph 1(4) is left out;

(*c*) in paragraph 6—

(i) in sub-paragraph (1) the words "in accordance with plans deposited" are left out; and

(ii) in sub-paragraph (2)—

(*aa*) the words ", on application being made for the appropriate variation of the licence," are inserted after the word "shall";

(*bb*) the words "plans aforesaid" are replaced by the words "requirements aforesaid"; and

(*cc*) the words "plans as modified with the approval of the authority" are replaced by the words "requirements as modified by the authority".

(*d*) at the end of paragraph 7, the following paragraphs are inserted:—

"*Further provisions relating to renewal and transfer of licences*

7A.—(1) Subject to paragraph 7B below, where, before the date of expiry of a licence granted under this Act, an application has been made for the renewal of that licence, the licence shall be deemed to remain in force, notwithstanding that the date of expiry of the licence has passed, until the determination of the application by the licensing authority or the withdrawal of the application.

(2) Subject to paragraph 7B below, where, before the date of expiry of a licence granted under this Act, an application has been made for the transfer of that licence, the licence shall be deemed to remain in force (with any necessary modifications) notwithstanding that the date of expiry of the licence has passed until the determination of the application by the licensing authority or the withdrawal of the application.

(3) Where an applicant for the transfer of a licence granted under this Act is carrying on at the premises in respect of which the licence was granted the functions to which the licence relates, "any necessary modifications" where those words appear in sub-paragraph (2) above, means the substitution for the name of the licence holder of the name of the applicant for the transfer of the licence and any other necessary modifications.

7B.—(1) The following provisions of this paragraph shall have effect as respects cases where, before the date of expiry of a licence granted under this Act, an application for renewal of the licence has been made ("a renewal case") or an application for transfer of the licence has been made ("a transfer case").

(2) If the application is not determined before the prospective expiry date, the licence shall not be deemed to remain in force under paragraph 7A(1) or paragraph 7A(2) of this Schedule, after that date and the application shall be deemed to be withdrawn on that date, unless before then the applicant pays the council a continuation fee.

(3) Where a continuation fee is paid in pursuance of sub-paragraph (2) of this paragraph in a renewal case, the applicant's application for renewal shall be deemed to be an application for renewal for a period of twelve months starting on the day following the prospective expiry date.

(4) Where a continuation fee is paid in pursuance of sub-paragraph (2) of this paragraph in a transfer case—

(*a*) the applicant shall be deemed to have made an application for the renewal of the licence for a period of twelve months starting on the day following the prospective expiry date;

(*b*) the Council shall determine the application for transfer and deemed application for renewal together; and

(*c*) in the following provisions of this paragraph, references to "the application" in a transfer case are references to the application for transfer and the application for renewal.

(5) If the application is not determined before the date of the expiry of the renewal period under sub-paragraph (3) or (4) of this paragraph, as the case may be, the licence shall not be deemed to remain in force under paragraph 7A(1) or 7A(2) of this Schedule, as the case may be, after that date and the application shall be deemed to be withdrawn on that date, unless before then the applicant pays the council a further continuation fee.

(6) Where a further continuation fee is paid in pursuance of sub-paragraph (5) of this paragraph, then—

(*a*) in a renewal case, the applicant's application for renewal shall be deemed to be an application for renewal for a period starting on the day following the date of the expiry of the renewal period under sub-paragraph (3) of this paragraph; and

(*b*) in a transfer case, the applicant's application so far as it is a deemed application for renewal shall be deemed to be an application for renewal for a period starting on the day following the date of the expiry of the renewal period under sub-paragraph (4) of this paragraph.

(7) A deemed application for renewal under paragraph (6) shall be for a period expiring—

(*a*) where the application is withdrawn, on the date of withdrawal;

(*b*) where the application is refused, on the date of the refusal;

(*c*) where the application is granted, on one or other of the following:—

(i) the date twelve months after the beginning of the period; or

(ii) such other date as may be specified by the Council when allowing the application.

(8) In this paragraph—

"the prospective expiry date" means—

(*a*) in a transfer case, the date on which the licence would have expired if the application for transfer had not been made; and

(*b*) in a renewal case, the date of the expiry of the period in respect of which the application for renewal of the licence was made;

"a continuation fee" is a fee of the same amount as the fee payable in respect of an application for renewal of a licence.

Power to prescribe standard terms, conditions and restrictions

7C.—(1) The licensing authority may make regulations prescribing standard conditions applicable to all, or any class of, licences which may be granted under this Act.

(2) Where the licensing authority have made regulations under this paragraph, every licence granted, renewed or transferred by them shall be deemed to have been so granted, renewed or transferred subject to any standard conditions except so far as they are excluded or amended in any particular case.".

Cinemas.
1985 c. 13.

25.—(1) The Cinemas Act 1985 applies in the area of a participating council in accordance with the following subsections.

(2) In section 1(2), the words "grant a licence under this section to such a person as they think fit" are replaced by the words "grant to an applicant and from time to time renew or transfer a licence" and the words "they may determine" are replaced by the words "they may so specify".

(3) Subsection 3(5) is left out.

(4) Subsection 3(6) is replaced by the following subsections:—

"(6) Subject to section 3A below, where, before the date of expiry of a licence, an application has been made for the renewal of that licence, the licence shall be deemed to remain in force, notwithstanding that the date of expiry of the licence has passed, until the determination of the application by the licensing authority or the withdrawal of the application.

(6A) Subject to section 3A below, where, before the date of expiry of a licence, an application has been made for the transfer of that licence, the licence shall be deemed to remain in force (with any necessary modifications) notwithstanding that the date of expiry of the licence has passed, until the determination of the application by the licensing authority or the withdrawal of the application.

(6B) Where an applicant for the transfer of a licence is carrying on at the premises in respect of which the licence was granted the functions to which the licence relates, "any necessary modifications" where those words appear in subsection (6A) above, means the substitution of the name of the licence holder by the name of the applicant for the transfer of the licence and any other necessary modifications.

(6C) Subject to section 4 below, the licensing authority may make regulations prescribing standard conditions applicable to all, or any class of, licences which may be granted by them.

(6D) Where the licensing authority have made regulations under subsection (6C) above, every licence granted, renewed or transferred by them shall be deemed to have been so granted, renewed or transferred subject to any standard conditions except so far as they are expressly excluded or amended in any particular case.

(6E) Where application is made to the licensing authority for the grant of a licence in respect of premises which are to be, or are in the course of being constructed, extended or altered and the licensing authority are satisfied that the premises would, if completed in accordance with the requirements of the licensing authority be such that they would grant the licence, the licensing authority may grant the licence subject to a condition that it shall be of no effect until confirmed by them.

(6F) The licensing authority shall on application being made for the appropriate variation of the licence confirm any licence granted by virtue of subsection (6E) above if and when they are satisfied that the premises have been completed in accordance with the requirements aforesaid or in accordance with those requirements as modified by the licensing authority and that the licence is held by a fit and proper person.".

(5) After section 3, the following section is inserted:—

"Renewal and transfer of licence: supplementary.

3A.—(1) The following provisions of this section shall have effect as respects cases where, before the date of expiry of a licence an application for renewal of the licence has been made ("a renewal case") or an application for transfer of the licence has been made ("a transfer case").

(2) If the application is not determined before the prospective expiry date, the licence shall not be deemed to remain in force under section 3(6) or section 3(6A) above in a transfer case, after that date and the application shall be deemed to be withdrawn on that date, unless before then the applicant pays the council a continuation fee.

(3) Where a continuation fee is paid in pursuance of subsection (2) above in a renewal case, the applicant's application for renewal shall be deemed to be an application for renewal for a period of twelve months starting on the day following the prospective expiry date.

(4) Where a continuation fee is paid in pursuance of subsection (2) of this section in a transfer case—

(*a*) the applicant shall be deemed to have made an application for the renewal of the licence for a period of twelve months starting on the day following the prospective expiry date;

(*b*) the Council shall determine the application for transfer and deemed application for renewal together; and

(*c*) in the following provisions of this section, references to "the application" in a transfer case are references to the application for transfer and the application for renewal.

(5) If the application is not determined before the date of the expiry of the renewal period under subsection (3) or (4) above, as the case may be, the licence shall not be deemed to remain in

force under section 3(6) or (6A) above, as the case may be, after that date, and the application shall be deemed to be withdrawn on that date, unless before then the applicant pays the council a further continuation fee.

(6) Where a further continuation fee is paid in pursuance of subsection (5) of this section, then—

(*a*) in a renewal case, the applicant's application for renewal shall be deemed to be an application for renewal for a period starting on the day following the date of the expiry of the renewal period under subsection (3) of this section; and

(*b*) in a transfer case, the applicant's application so far as it is a deemed application for renewal shall be deemed to be an application for renewal for a period starting on the day following the date of the expiry of the renewal period under subsection (4) of this section.

(7) A deemed application for renewal under subsection (6) shall be for a period expiring—

(*a*) where the application is withdrawn, on the date of withdrawal;

(*b*) where the application is refused, on the date of the refusal;

(*c*) where the application is granted, on one or other of the following:—

(i) the date twelve months after the beginning of the period; or

(ii) such other date as may be specified by the Council when allowing the application.

(8) In this section—

"the prospective expiry date" means—

(*a*) in a transfer case, the date on which the licence would have expired if the application for transfer had not been made; and

(*b*) in a renewal case, the date of the expiry of the period in respect of which the application for renewal of the licence was made;

"a continuation fee" is a fee of the same amount as the fee payable in respect of an application for renewal of a licence.".

(6) In subsection (2) of section 10 after paragraph (*c*) the following paragraph is inserted:—

"(*cc*) an applicant for the transfer of a licence where he is carrying out the functions to which the licence relates;".

(7) In section 16 at the beginning of subsections (4) and (5) the words "Subject to section 16A below" are inserted.

(8) After the said section 16, the following section is inserted:—

"Appeals: supplementary provisions.   **16A.**—(1) The following provisions of this section shall have effect as respects cases where an appeal under section 16 above is brought, within the period for doing so, against the revocation of a licence ("a revocation case") or against the refusal of an application for renewal of a licence ("a refusal case").

(2) If the appeal is not determined before the prospective expiry date, the licence shall not be deemed to remain in force under section 16(4) or (5) above after that date, and the appeal shall be deemed to be abandoned on that date, unless before then—

(a) in a revocation case, the appellant makes an application for the renewal of the licence for a period of twelve months starting on the day following the prospective expiry date;

(b) in a refusal case the appellant pays the council a continuation fee.

(3) Where a continuation fee is paid in pursuance of subsection (2)(b) above, the appellant's refused application for renewal shall be deemed to be an application for renewal for a period of twelve months starting on the day following the prospective expiry date.

(4) If the appeal is not determined before the date of the expiry of the renewal period under subsection (2)(a) or (3) above, as the case may be, the licence shall not be deemed to remain in force under section 16(4) or (5) of this Act after that date, and the appeal shall be deemed to be abandoned on that date, unless before then the appellant pays the council a continuation fee or, as the case may be, a further continuation fee.

(5) Where a continuation fee or a further continuation fee is paid in pursuance of subsection (4) above, the appellant's application for renewal or, as the case may be, refused application for renewal shall be deemed to be an application for renewal for a period starting on the day following the date of the expiry of the renewal period under subsection (2)(a) above or, as the case may be, subsection (3) above.

(6) A deemed application for renewal under subsection (5) shall be for a period expiring—

(a) where the appeal is withdrawn, on the date of withdrawal;

(b) where the appeal is unsuccessful—

(i) if a further appeal is available but is not made within the period for doing so, on the date of the expiry of that period;

(ii) if no further appeal is available, on the date of the decision of the court;

(c) where the appeal is successful, on the day before the date of the next anniversary of the beginning of the period; provided that where the period, at the time of the decision of the court, has been running for more than twelve months, the court may specify an earlier date.

(7) In this section—

"the prospective expiry date" means—

(a) in a revocation case, the date on which the licence would have expired if it had not been revoked; and

(b) in a refusal case, the date of the expiry of the period in respect of which the refused application for renewal of the licence was made;

"a continuation fee" is a fee of the same amount as the fee payable in respect of an application for renewal of a licence.".

Night cafés.
1990 c. vii.

26.—(1) Part II of the London Local Authorities Act 1990 (Night Café Licensing) applies in the area of a participating council in accordance with the following subsections.

(2) In section 7 (Applications)—

(a) in subsection (7)—

(i) at the beginning, the words "Subject to section 7A (Renewal and transfer of licence: supplementary) of this Act," are inserted;

(ii) the words "or transfer" and the words "or as the case may require, to have effect with any necessary modifications" are left out;

(b) at the end the following subsections are inserted:—

"(8) Subject to section 7A (Renewal and transfer of licence: supplementary) of this Act, where, before the date of expiry of a night café licence, an application has been made for the transfer of that licence, the licence shall be deemed to remain in force (with any necessary modifications) notwithstanding that the date of expiry of the licence has passed, until the determination of the application by the council or the withdrawal of the application.

(9) Where an applicant for the transfer of a night café licence is carrying on the functions to which the licence relates, "any necessary modifications" where those words appear in subsection (8) above, means the substitution for the name of the licence holder by the name of the applicant for the transfer of the licence and any other necessary modifications.".

(3) After the said section 7, the following section is inserted:—

"Renewal and transfer of licence: supplementary.   **7A.**—(1) The following provisions of this section shall have effect as respects cases where, before the date of expiry of a licence an application for renewal of the licence has been made ("a renewal case") or an application for transfer of the licence has been made ("a transfer case").

(2) If the application is not determined before the prospective expiry date, the licence shall not be deemed to remain in force under subsection (7) or (8) of section 7 (Applications) of this Act, after that date and the application shall be deemed to be withdrawn on that date, unless before then the applicant pays the council a continuation fee.

(3) Where a continuation fee is paid in pursuance of subsection (2) above in a renewal case, the applicant's application for renewal shall be deemed to be an application for renewal for a period of twelve months starting on the day following the prospective expiry date.

(4) Where a continuation fee is paid in pursuance of subsection (2) above in a transfer case—

   (*a*) the applicant shall be deemed to have made an application for the renewal of the licence for a period of twelve months starting on the day following the prospective expiry date;

   (*b*) the Council shall determine the application for transfer and deemed application for renewal together; and

   (*c*) in the following provisions of this section, references to "the application" in a transfer case are references to the application for transfer and the application for renewal.

(5) If the application is not determined before the date of the expiry of the renewal period under subsection (3) or (4) above, as the case may be, the licence shall not be deemed to remain in force under subsection (7) or (8) of the said section 7, as the case may be, after that date, and the application shall be deemed to be withdrawn on that date, unless before then the applicant pays the council a further continuation fee.

(6) Where a further continuation fee is paid in pursuance of subsection (5) above, then—

   (*a*) in a renewal case, the applicant's application for renewal shall be deemed to be an application for renewal for a period starting on the day following the date of the expiry of the renewal period under subsection (3) above; and

   (*b*) in a transfer case, the applicant's application so far as it is a deemed application for renewal shall be deemed to be an application for renewal for a period starting on the day following the date of the expiry of the renewal period under subsection (4) above.

(7) A deemed application for renewal under subsection (6) above shall be for a period expiring—

   (*a*) where the application is withdrawn, on the date of withdrawal;

   (*b*) where the application is refused, on the date of the refusal;

   (*c*) where the application is granted, on one or other of the following:—

   (i) the date twelve months after the beginning of the period; or

   (ii) such other date as may be specified by the Council when allowing the application.

(8) In this section—

"the prospective expiry date" means—

   (*a*) in a transfer case, the date on which the licence would have expired if the application for transfer had not been made; and

   (*b*) in a renewal case, the date of the expiry of the period in respect of which the application for renewal of the licence was made;

"a continuation fee" is a fee of the same amount as the fee payable in respect of an application for renewal of a licence.".

(4) In section 11 (Provisional grant of night café licences)—

   (*a*) in subsection (1) the words "in accordance with plans deposited" are left out; and

   (*b*) in subsection (2)—

      (i) the words "plans referred to in the said subsection (1)" are replaced by the words "requirements aforesaid"; and

      (ii) the words "plans as modified with the approval of the council" are replaced with the words "requirements as modified by the council".

(5) In section 14 (Appeals) at the beginning of subsection (5) the words "Subject to section 14A below" are inserted.

(6) After section 14, the following section is inserted:—

"Appeals: supplementary provisions.   **14A.**—(1) The following provisions of this section shall have effect as respects cases where an appeal under section 14 (Appeals) of this Act is brought, within the period for doing so, against the revocation of a licence ("a revocation case") or against the refusal of an application for renewal of a licence ("a refusal case").

(2) If the appeal is not determined before the prospective expiry date, the licence shall not be deemed to remain in force under subsection (5) of the said section 14 after that date, and the appeal shall be deemed to be abandoned on that date, unless before then—

   (*a*) in a revocation case, the appellant makes an application for the renewal of the licence for a period of twelve months starting on the day following the prospective expiry date;

   (*b*) in a refusal case the appellant pays the council a continuation fee.

(3) Where a continuation fee is paid in pursuance of subsection (2)(*b*) above, the appellant's refused application for renewal shall be deemed to be an application for renewal for a period of twelve months starting on the day following the prospective expiry date.

(4) If the appeal is not determined before the date of the expiry of the renewal period under subsection (2)(*a*) or (3) above, as the case may be, the licence shall not be deemed to remain in force under the said section 14 after that date, and the appeal shall be deemed to be abandoned on that date, unless before then the appellant pays the council a continuation fee or, as the case may be, a further continuation fee.

(5) Where a continuation fee or a further continuation fee is paid in pursuance of subsection (4) above, the appellant's application for renewal or, as the case may be, refused application for renewal shall be deemed to be an application for renewal for a period starting on the day following the date of the expiry of the

renewal period under subsection (2)(*a*) above or, as the case may be, subsection (3) above.

(6) A deemed application for renewal under subsection (5) shall be for a period expiring—

> (*a*) where the appeal is withdrawn, on the date of withdrawal;

> (*b*) where the appeal is unsuccessful—

>> (i) if a further appeal is available but is not made within the period for doing so, on the date of the expiry of that period;

>> (ii) if no further appeal is available, on the date of the decision of the court;

> (*c*) where the appeal is successful, on the day before the date of the next anniversary of the beginning of the period; provided that where the period, at the time of the decision of the court, has been running for more than twelve months, the court may specify an earlier date.

(7) In this section—

"the prospective expiry date" means—

>> (*a*) in a revocation case, the date on which the licence would have expired if it had not been revoked; and

>> (*b*) in a refusal case, the date of the expiry of the period in respect of which the refused application for renewal of the licence was made;

> "a continuation fee" is a fee of the same amount as the fee payable in respect of an application for renewal of a licence.".

(7) In subsection (2) of section 15 (Enforcement) after the words "holder of the licence" the words ", an applicant for the transfer of a licence where he is carrying out the functions to which the licence relates;" are inserted.

27.—(1) Part II (Special Treatment Premises) of the London Local Authorities Act 1991 applies in the area of a participating council other than the City in accordance with the following subsections.

(2) In section 4 (Interpretation of Part II)—

> (*a*) the exception from the definition of "establishment for special treatment" provided in paragraph (*b*)(ii) of the definition shall not apply to any premises in which the member of the body of health practitioners concerned also carries out, or supervises the carrying out of, therapy not requiring any qualifications as are mentioned in paragraph (*b*)(ii)(B) of the definition unless by reason of the carrying out, or supervision of the carrying out, of such therapy the premises would on other grounds fall outside the definition of establishment for special treatment;

> (*b*) in paragraph (*b*), at the end of sub-paragraph (iii), the following sub-paragraphs are inserted:—

>> "(iv) in the case of osteopathy, a person registered as a fully registered osteopath or a conditionally registered osteopath under the Osteopaths Act 1993;

Special treatment premises.
1991 c. xiii.

1993 c. 21.

(v) in the case of chiropractic, a person registered as a fully registered chiropractor or a conditionally registered chiropractor under the Chiropractors Act 1994;";

(*c*) at the end of the said definition, the following paragraph is inserted:—

"(*f*) any premises where the only special treatment carried out is of a class which from time to time is by resolution of the borough council excluded from the operation of this Part of this Act;";

(*d*) after the definition of "establishment for special treatment" the following definition is inserted:—

"'health practitioner' means a person who uses his skills with a view to the curing or alleviating of bodily diseases or ailments but does not include a person whose skills are employed mainly for cosmetic alteration or decorative purposes;".

(3) In section 7 (Applications under Part II)—

(*a*) in subsection (7)—

(i) at the beginning the words "Subject to section 7A (Renewal and transfer of licence: supplementary) of this Act," are inserted;

(ii) the words "or transfer" and the words "or, as the case may require, to have effect with any necessary modifications" are left out;

(*b*) at the end the following subsections are inserted:—

"(8) Subject to section 7A (Renewal and transfer of licence: supplementary) of this Act, where, before the date of expiry of a licence, an application has been made for the transfer of that licence, the licence shall be deemed to remain in force (with any necessary modifications) notwithstanding that the date of expiry of the licence has passed.

(9) Where an applicant for the transfer of a licence is carrying on the functions to which the licence relates, "any necessary modifications" where those words appear in subsection (8) above, means the substitution for the name of the licence holder of the name of the applicant for the transfer of the licence and any other necessary modifications.".

(4) After the said section 7, the following section is inserted:—

"Renewal and transfer of licence: supplementary.

7A.—(1) The following provisions of this section shall have effect as respects cases where, before the date of expiry of a licence an application for renewal of the licence has been made ("a renewal case") or an application for transfer of the licence has been made ("a transfer case").

(2) If the application is not determined before the prospective expiry date, the licence shall not be deemed to remain in force under subsection (7) or (8) of section 7 (Applications) of this Act, after that date and the application shall be deemed to be withdrawn on that date, unless before then the applicant pays the council a continuation fee.

(3) Where a continuation fee is paid in pursuance of subsection (2) above in a renewal case, the applicant's application for renewal shall be deemed to be an application for renewal for a period of twelve months starting on the day following the prospective expiry date.

(4) Where a continuation fee is paid in pursuance of subsection (2) above in a transfer case—

(*a*) the applicant shall be deemed to have made an application for the renewal of the licence for a period of twelve months starting on the day following the prospective expiry date;

(*b*) the Council shall determine the application for transfer and deemed application for renewal together; and

(*c*) in the following provisions of this section, references to "the application" in a transfer case are references to the application for transfer and the application for renewal.

(5) If the application is not determined before the date of the expiry of the renewal period under subsection (3) or (4) above, as the case may be, the licence shall not be deemed to remain in force under subsection (7) or (8) of the said section 7, as the case may be, after that date, and the application shall be deemed to be withdrawn on that date, unless before then the applicant pays the council a further continuation fee.

(6) Where a further continuation fee is paid in pursuance of subsection (5) above, then—

(*a*) in a renewal case, the applicant's application for renewal shall be deemed to be an application for renewal for a period starting on the day following the date of the expiry of the renewal period under subsection (3) above; and

(*b*) in a transfer case, the applicant's application so far as it is a deemed application for renewal shall be deemed to be an application for renewal for a period starting on the day following the date of the expiry of the renewal period under subsection (4) above.

(7) A deemed application for renewal under subsection (6) shall be for a period expiring—

(*a*) where the application is withdrawn, on the date of withdrawal;

(*b*) where the application is refused, on the date of the refusal;

(*c*) where the application is granted, on one or other of the following:—

(i) the date twelve months after the beginning of the period; or

(ii) such other date as may be specified by the Council when allowing the application.

(8) In this section—

"the prospective expiry date" means—

(*a*) in a transfer case, the date on which the licence would have expired if the application for transfer had not been made; and

(*b*) in a renewal case, the date of the expiry of the period in respect of which the application for renewal of the licence was made;

"a continuation fee" is a fee of the same amount as the fee payable in respect of an application for renewal of a licence.".

(5) In section 13 (Part II appeals) at the beginning of subsection (5) the words "Subject to section 13A below" are inserted.

(6) After the said section 13, the following section is inserted:—

"Appeals: supplementary provisions.

13A.—(1) The following provisions of this section shall have effect as respects cases where an appeal under section 13 (Part II appeals) of this Act is brought, within the period for doing so, against the revocation of a licence ("a revocation case") or against the refusal of an application for renewal of a licence ("a refusal case").

(2) If the appeal is not determined before the prospective expiry date, the licence shall not be deemed to remain in force under subsection (5) of the said section 13 after that date, and the appeal shall be deemed to be abandoned on that date, unless before then—

(*a*) in a revocation case, the appellant makes an application for the renewal of the licence for a period of twelve months starting on the day following the prospective expiry date;

(*b*) in a refusal case the appellant pays the council a continuation fee.

(3) Where a continuation fee is paid in pursuance of subsection (2)(*b*) above, the appellant's refused application for renewal shall be deemed to be an application for renewal for a period of twelve months starting on the day following the prospective expiry date.

(4) If the appeal is not determined before the date of the expiry of the renewal period under subsection (2)(*a*) or (3) above, as the case may be, the licence shall not be deemed to remain in force under subsection (5) of the said section 13 after that date, and the appeal shall be deemed to be abandoned on that date, unless before then the appellant pays the council a continuation fee or, as the case may be, a further continuation fee.

(5) Where a continuation fee or a further continuation fee is paid in pursuance of subsection (4) above, the appellant's application for renewal or, as the case may be, refused application for renewal shall be deemed to be an application for renewal for a period starting on the day following the date of the expiry of the renewal period under subsection (2)(*a*) above or, as the case may be, subsection (3) above.

(6) A deemed application for renewal under subsection (5) shall be for a period expiring—

(*a*) where the appeal is withdrawn, on the date of withdrawal;

(*b*) where the appeal is unsuccessful—

(i) if a further appeal is available, but is not made within the period for doing so, on the date of the expiry of that period;

(ii) if no further appeal is available, on the date of the decision of the court;

(c) where the appeal is successful, on the day before the date of the next anniversary of the beginning of the period; provided that where the period, at the time of the decision of the court, has been running for more than twelve months, the court may specify an earlier date.

(7) In this section—

"the prospective expiry date" means—

(a) in a revocation case, the date on which the licence would have expired if it had not been revoked; and

(b) in a refusal case, the date of the expiry of the period in respect of which the refused application for renewal of the licence was made;

"a continuation fee" is a fee of the same amount as the fee payable in respect of an application for renewal of a licence.".

(7) In subsection (2) of section 14 (Enforcement of Part II) after the words "holder of the licence" the words ", an applicant for the transfer of a licence where he is carrying out the functions to which the licence relates" are inserted.

28.—(1) In the case where Part II (Special Treatment Premises) of the London Local Authorities Act 1991 (in this section referred to as "the Act of 1991") applies to a participating borough on the date on which this Act is passed this section shall come into operation at the end of the period of three months beginning with that date and where Part II of the Act of 1991 does not so apply shall come into operation on the date from which it first applies to a participating borough.

Application of Part II of Act of 1991 to existing special treatment premises.
1991 c. xiii.

(2) After the expiry of the period of four weeks beginning with the date this section comes into force in a borough, subsection (3) of section 16 (Application to existing special treatment premises) of the Act of 1991 ceases to have effect in that borough and where premises to which subsection (1) of that section does not apply are lawfully being used as an establishment for special treatment, section 6 (Licensing under Part II) of the Act of 1991 has effect in relation to those premises.

(3) Where premises to which subsection (1) of the said section 16 does not apply are lawfully being used as an establishment for special treatment on the date this section comes into force in the borough in which the premises are situated and application for a licence under Part II of the Act of 1991 is made within four weeks of that date those premises may lawfully continue to be used as an establishment for special treatment until the determination or withdrawal of that application and if an appeal is lodged until the determination or abandonment of the appeal.

29.—(1) Part IV (Near Beer Licensing) of the London Local Authorities Act 1995 applies in the area of a participating council in accordance with the following subsections.

Near beer premises.
1995 c. x.

(2) In section 14 (Interpretation of Part IV)—

(*a*) in the definition of "near beer premises" paragraph (*a*) is replaced by the following paragraph:—

"(*a*) consists in or includes the sale to customers for consumption on the premises of refreshments; and"

(*b*) the definition of "occupier" is left out.

(3) In section 17 (Applications under Part IV)—

(*a*) in subsection (1) the words from the beginning to "and shall" are replaced by "An applicant for the grant, renewal or transfer of a near beer licence shall";

(*b*) in subsection (7)—

(i) at the beginning, the words "Subject to section 17A (Renewal and transfer of licence: supplementary) of this Act," are inserted;

(ii) the words "or transfer" and the words from "or as the case may require, to have effect with any necessary modifications" are left out;

(*c*) at the end the following subsections are inserted:—

"(8) Subject to section 17A (Renewal and transfer of licence: supplementary) of this Act, where, before the date of expiry of a near beer licence, an application has been made for the transfer of that licence, the licence shall be deemed to remain in force (with any necessary modifications) notwithstanding that the date of expiry of the licence has passed, until the determination of the application by the council or the withdrawal of the application.

(9) Where an applicant for the transfer of a near beer licence is carrying on the functions to which the licence relates, "any necessary modifications" where those words appear in subsection (8) above, means the substitution for the name of the licence holder of the name of the applicant for the transfer of the licence and any other necessary modifications.".

(4) After the said section 17, the following section is inserted:—

"Renewal and transfer of licence: supplementary. **17A.**—(1) The following provisions of this section shall have effect as respects cases where, before the date of expiry of a licence an application for renewal of the licence has been made ("a renewal case") or an application for transfer of the licence has been made ("a transfer case").

(2) If the application is not determined before the prospective expiry date, the licence shall not be deemed to remain in force under subsection (7) or (8) of section 17 (Applications) of this Act, after that date and the application shall be deemed to be withdrawn on that date, unless before then the applicant pays the council a continuation fee.

(3) Where a continuation fee is paid in pursuance of subsection (2) above in a renewal case, the applicant's application for renewal shall be deemed to be an application for renewal for a period of twelve months starting on the day following the prospective expiry date.

(4) Where a continuation fee is paid in pursuance of subsection (2) above in a transfer case—

(*a*) the applicant shall be deemed to have made an application for the renewal of the licence for a period of twelve months starting on the day following the prospective expiry date;

(*b*) the Council shall determine the application for transfer and deemed application for renewal together; and

(*c*) in the following provisions of this section, references to "the application" in a transfer case are references to the application for transfer and the application for renewal.

(5) If the application is not determined before the date of the expiry of the renewal period under subsection (3) or (4) above, as the case may be, the licence shall not be deemed to remain in force under subsection (7) or (8) of the said section 17, as the case may be, after that date, and the application shall be deemed to be withdrawn on that date, unless before then the applicant pays the council a further continuation fee.

(6) Where a further continuation fee is paid in pursuance of subsection (5) above then—

(*a*) in a renewal case, the applicant's application for renewal shall be deemed to be an application for renewal for a period starting on the day following the date of the expiry of the renewal period under subsection (3) above; and

(*b*) in a transfer case, the applicant's application so far as it is a deemed application for renewal shall be deemed to be an application for renewal for a period starting on the day following the date of the expiry of the renewal period under subsection (4) above.

(7) A deemed application for renewal under subsection (6) shall be for a period expiring—

(*a*) where the application is withdrawn, on the date of withdrawal;

(*b*) where the application is refused, on the date of the refusal;

(*c*) where the application is granted, on one or other of the following:—

(i) the date twelve months after the beginning of the period; or

(ii) such other date as may be specified by the Council when allowing the application.

(8) In this section—

"the prospective expiry date" means—

(*a*) in a transfer case, the date on which the licence would have expired if the application for transfer had not been made; and

(*b*) in a renewal case, the date of the expiry of the period in respect of which the application for renewal of the licence was made;

"a continuation fee" is a fee of the same amount as the fee payable in respect of an application for renewal of a licence.".

PART IV
—*cont.*

(5) In section 23 (Appeals under Part IV) at the beginning of subsection (5) the words "Subject to section 23A below" are inserted.

(6) After the said section 23, the following section is inserted:—

"Appeals: supplementary provisions.

23A.—(1) The following provisions of this section shall have effect as respects cases where an appeal under section 23 (Appeals under Part IV) of this Act is brought, within the period for doing so, against the revocation of a licence ("a revocation case") or against the refusal of an application for renewal of a licence ("a refusal case").

(2) If the appeal is not determined before the prospective expiry date, the licence shall not be deemed to remain in force under subsection (5) of the said section 23 after that date, and the appeal shall be deemed to be abandoned on that date, unless before then—

> (*a*) in a revocation case, the appellant makes an application for the renewal of the licence for a period of twelve months starting on the day following the prospective expiry date;

> (*b*) in a refusal case the appellant pays the council a continuation fee.

(3) Where a continuation fee is paid in pursuance of subsection (2)(*b*) above, the appellant's refused application for renewal shall be deemed to be an application for renewal for a period of twelve months starting on the day following the prospective expiry date.

(4) If the appeal is not determined before the date of the expiry of the renewal period under subsection (2)(*a*) or (3) above, as the case may be, the licence shall not be deemed to remain in force under subsection (5) of the said section 23 after that date, and the appeal shall be deemed to be abandoned on that date, unless before then the appellant pays the council a continuation fee or, as the case may be, a further continuation fee.

(5) Where a continuation fee or a further continuation fee is paid in pursuance of subsection (4) above, the appellant's application for renewal or, as the case may be, refused application for renewal shall be deemed to be an application for renewal for a period starting on the day following the date of the expiry of the renewal period under subsection (2)(*a*) above or, as the case may be, subsection (3) above.

(6) A deemed application for renewal under subsection (5) shall be for a period expiring—

> (*a*) where the appeal is withdrawn, on the date of withdrawal;

> (*b*) where the appeal is unsuccessful—

>> (i) if a further appeal is available but is not made within the period for doing so, on the date of the expiry of that period;

>> (ii) if no further appeal is available, on the date of the decision of the court;

> (*c*) where the appeal is successful, on the day before the date of the next anniversary of the beginning of the period;

provided that where the period, at the time of the
decision of the court, has been running for more than
twelve months, the court may specify an earlier date.

(7) In this section—

"the prospective expiry date" means—

(*a*) in a revocation case, the date on which the
licence would have expired if it had not been
revoked; and

(*b*) in a refusal case, the date of the expiry of the
period in respect of which the refused
application for renewal of the licence was made;

"a continuation fee" is a fee of the same amount as the fee
payable in respect of an application for renewal of a
licence.".

(7) In subsection (2) of section 24 (Enforcement under Part IV) after the
words "holder of the licence" the words ", an applicant for the transfer of a
near beer licence where he is carrying out the functions to which the
licence relates" are inserted.

30. In its application to the area of a participating council, section 29
(Interpretation of Part V) of the London Local Authorities Act 1995 is
amended as follows—

Door
supervisors.
1995 c. x.

(*a*) in paragraph (*c*) of the definition of "licensed premises" the words
"or licensed" are left out;

(*b*) in the definition of "door supervisor"—

(i) before the words "to maintain order" the words "any
person employed" are inserted; and

(ii) at the end the words "but, in respect of premises in
respect of which there is in force for the time being a justices'
on-licence within the meaning of section 1(2) of the Licensing
Act 1964 does not include the holder of that licence" are
inserted.

1964 c. 26.

31. Subsection (6) of section 4 (Distribution of free literature) of the
London Local Authorities Act 1994 is amended in its application to the
area of a participating council other than the City by the substitution of the
words "in whole or in part the reasonable administrative or other costs in
connection with their functions under this section" for the words "the
expense of the borough council in dealing with applications for such
consents".

Fees in relation
to distribution of
free literature.
1994 c. xii.

PART V

LICENSING OF BUSKERS

32. In this Part of this Act—

Interpretation of
Part V.

"busking" means the provision of entertainment in a street but does not
include the provision of entertainment—

(*a*) of a class which from time to time is by resolution of a
participating council excluded from the operation of this
Part of this Act;

(*b*) under and in accordance with the terms of a licence granted under paragraph 1 of Schedule 12 to the London Government Act 1963;

(*c*) which is authorised specifically to take place in a street under any other enactment; or

(*d*) consisting of music performed as an incident of a religious meeting, procession or service;

and "busk" and "busks" shall be construed accordingly;

"licence" means a licence under section 35 (Power to license) of this Act and "licensed" shall be construed accordingly;

"street" includes—

(*a*) any street or way to which the public commonly have access, whether or not as of right;

(*b*) any place, not being within permanently enclosed premises, within 7 metres of any such street or way, to which the public commonly have access;

(*c*) any area in the open air to which the public commonly have access;

(*d*) any street, way or open area within any housing development provided or maintained by a local authority under Part II of the Housing Act 1985;

but does not include any land in respect of which there are byelaws in force which regulate the provision of entertainment and which are made by London Transport Executive or London Regional Transport.

33.—(1) This Part of this Act applies in the area of a participating council as from such day as may be fixed in relation to that council by resolution, and the council may apply this Part to all their area or to any part identified in the resolution and notice under this section.

(2) The council shall not pass a resolution under this section in respect of any part of their area unless they have reason to believe that there has been, is being or is likely to be caused, as a result of busking—

(*a*) undue interference with or inconvenience to or risk to safety of persons using a street in that part of their area or other streets within the vicinity of that street; or

(*b*) nuisance to the occupiers of property in or in the vicinity of a street in that part of their area.

(3) The council shall cause to be published in a local newspaper circulating in the borough or the City notice—

(*a*) of the passing of any such resolution and of a day fixed thereby; and

(*b*) of the general effect of the provisions of this Act coming into operation as from that day;

and the day so fixed shall not be earlier than the expiration of three months from the publication of the said notice.

(4) Either a photostatic or other reproduction certified by the officer appointed for that purpose by the council to be a true reproduction of a page or part of a page of any such newspaper bearing the date of its publication and containing any such notice shall be evidence of the publication of the notice, and of the date of publication.

PART V
—*cont.*

34. If a participating council consider that busking should be licensed in their area they may pass any of the following resolutions:—

Designation of licence streets.

(*a*) a resolution (in this Part of this Act referred to as a "designating resolution") designating any street or part of a street within the borough or the City as a "licence street";

(*b*) a resolution prescribing in relation to any licence street or any part of a licence street any hours during which busking may take place;

and may by subsequent resolution rescind or vary any such resolution.

35.—(1) The council may license an applicant for one or more days or such period as may be specified in the licence on such terms and conditions and subject to such restrictions as may be so specified.

Power to license.

(2) Without prejudice to the generality of subsection (1) above, such conditions may relate to—

(*a*) the area in which busking may take place;

(*b*) the hours during which busking may take place;

(*c*) the prevention of obstruction to persons using the street; or

(*d*) the prevention of nuisance to the occupiers of nearby property.

36.—(1) An applicant for the grant of a licence shall provide such information as the council may by regulation prescribe.

Applicants under Part V.

(2) Regulations under subsection (1) above may, inter alia, prescribe the procedure for determining applications.

(3) An applicant for a licence shall pay such fee determined by the council as may be sufficient to cover in whole or in part the reasonable administrative or other costs incurred in connection with their functions under this Part of this Act.

37.—(1) The council may refuse to grant a licence on any of the following grounds:—

Refusal of licence.

(*a*) that the applicant could be reasonably regarded as not being a fit and proper person to hold a licence;

(*b*) that there is not enough space in the street in respect of which the application is made for busking to take place without causing undue interference with, or inconvenience to, or risk to the safety of persons using the street, or other streets within the vicinity of the street;

(*c*) that there is a likelihood of nuisance being caused to the occupiers of premises in or in the vicinity of the street in respect of which the application is made.

(2) The council shall refuse to grant a licence in respect of an application which relates to any street other than a licence street.

38. The council may, at the written request of the holder of a licence, cancel that licence.

Cancellation of licence.

Revocation of
licence.

39. The council may revoke a licence on any of the following grounds:—

(*a*) that there has been a breach of the conditions of the licence;

(*b*) that undue interference with, or inconvenience to, or risk to the safety of persons using the street, or other streets within the vicinity of the street, has been caused as a result of the busking;

(*c*) that nuisance has been caused as a result of the busking to occupiers of property in or in the vicinity of the street in respect of which the licence was granted.

Power to
prescribe
standard terms,
conditions and
restrictions
under Part V.

40.—(1) The council may make regulations prescribing standard conditions applicable to all licences.

(2) Where the council have made regulations under this section, every licence granted by them shall be deemed to have been so granted subject to the standard conditions except so far as they are expressly excluded or amended in any particular case.

(3) Without prejudice to the generality of subsection (1) above, the standard conditions applied shall include a condition requiring the licence holder to carry his licence with him when busking.

Appeals under
Part V.

41.—(1) Any of the following persons, that is to say:—

(*a*) an applicant for the grant of a licence whose application is refused;

(*b*) a licence holder who is aggrieved by any term, condition or restriction on or subject to which the licence is held; or

(*c*) a licence holder whose licence has been revoked;

may at any time before the expiration of the period of 21 days beginning with the relevant date appeal to the magistrates' court acting for the area in which the licence street is situated by way of complaint for an order.

(2) In subsection (1) above "the relevant date" means either the date on which the person in question or his representative is informed in writing of the refusal of his application, the imposition of the terms, conditions or restrictions by which he is aggrieved or the revocation of his registration, as the case may be, or 7 days after the date when such notification was posted to him by first class pre-paid letter, whichever is the earlier.

(3) An appeal by either party against the decision of the magistrates' court under this section may be made to the Crown Court.

(4) On an appeal to the magistrates' court or to the Crown Court under this section the court may make such order as it thinks fit in relation to the matter which is the subject of the appeal and it shall be the duty of the council to give effect to such order.

Enforcement
under Part V.

42. Any person who—

(*a*) busks in any street to which this Part of this Act applies without the authority of a licence; or

(*b*) is concerned with the organisation or management of busking which is not authorised by a licence; or

(*c*) contravenes any condition of his licence; or

(*d*) in connection with his application for a licence makes a statement which he knows to be false in a material particular;

shall be guilty of an offence and shall be liable on summary conviction to a fine not exceeding level 3 on the standard scale.

43.—(1) An authorised officer or a constable who has reasonable cause to believe that busking is taking place or is about to take place without a licence or in breach of the terms and conditions of a licence or in a street which is not a licence street to which this Part of this Act applies may require that busking either cease or not take place.

(2) Subject to subsection (3) below if the busking continues or takes place despite the requirement under subsection (1) above the authorised officer or constable may seize and remove any apparatus or equipment used in connection with the busking which may be required to be used in evidence in respect of an offence under section 42 (Enforcement under Part V) of this Act.

(3) An authorised officer or constable shall not seize any apparatus or equipment in pursuance of the powers in subsection (2) above unless the person busking fails to produce, in pursuance of a request by the constable or authorised officer, a licence authorising the busking.

(4) Before exercising any power under this section, an authorised officer shall, if requested to do so by the person busking, produce his authority.

(5) (*a*) The following provisions of this subsection shall have effect where any apparatus or equipment or any other thing is seized by an authorised officer under subsection (2) above and reference in those provisions to proceedings are to proceedings in respect of the alleged offence in relation to which the apparatus or equipment is seized.

(*b*) Subject to paragraph (*c*) below, after the conclusion of the proceedings, the apparatus or equipment shall be returned to the person from whom it was seized unless—

    (i) the court orders it to be forfeited under any enactment;

    (ii) any costs awarded to the council by the court, have not been paid within 28 days of the making of the order.

(*c*) Where after 28 days any costs awarded by the court to the council have not been paid to the council in full, the apparatus or equipment may be disposed of in any way the council thinks fit and any sum obtained by the council in excess of the costs awarded by the court shall be returned to the person to whom the apparatus or equipment belongs and when any apparatus or equipment is disposed of by the council under this subsection the council shall have a duty to secure the best possible price which can reasonably be obtained for that apparatus or equipment.

(*d*) If no proceedings are instituted before the expiration of a period of 28 days beginning with the date of seizure, or any proceedings instituted within that period are discontinued, at the expiration of that period or, as the case may be, on the discontinuance of the proceedings, the apparatus or equipment shall, subject to paragraph (*e*) below, be returned to the person from whom it was seized unless it has not proved possible, after diligent enquiry, to identify that person and ascertain his address.

(*e*) Where the apparatus or equipment is not returned because it has not proved possible to identify the person from whom it was seized and ascertain his address, the council (whether the article or thing was seized by an authorised officer or a constable) may apply to a magistrates' court for an order as to the manner in which it should be dealt with.

(6) In this section "authorised officer" includes a person employed by any contractor of the council with whom the council has contracted for the

purposes of this section where that person has been authorised in writing by that contractor to act in relation to this section.

(7) (*a*) This subsection shall have effect where apparatus or equipment is seized under subsection (2) above and either—

  (i) not less than six months have passed since the date of the seizure and no information has been laid against any person for an offence under this section in respect of the act or circumstances which occasioned the seizure; or

  (ii) proceedings for such an offence have been brought and either the person charged has been acquitted (whether or not on appeal) and the time for appealing against or challenging the acquittal (where applicable) has expired without an appeal or challenge being brought, or the proceedings (including any appeal) have been withdrawn by, or have failed for want of prosecution by, the person by whom the original proceedings were brought.

(*b*) When this subsection has effect a person who has or at the time of seizure had a legal interest in the apparatus or equipment seized may recover compensation from the council or (where it is seized by a constable) the Commissioner by civil action in the County Court in respect of any loss suffered by him as a result of the seizure.

(*c*) The court may only make an order for compensation under paragraph (*b*) above if satisfied that seizure was not lawful under subsection (2) above.

44.—(1) The following provisions shall have effect in relation to any resolution under section 34 (Designation of licence streets) of this Act.

(2) If a council pass a resolution, the resolution shall take effect on the day specified in the resolution (which must not be before the expiration of the period of one month beginning with the day on which the resolution is passed).

(3) A council shall not pass a resolution or rescind or vary a resolution unless—

  (*a*) they have published notice of their intention to do so in a local newspaper circulating in their area;

  (*b*) they have served a copy of the notice on—

      (i) the highway authority (unless they are the highway authority);

      (ii) the Commissioner;

      (iii) to any body which appears to the council to be representative of persons carrying on busking in the area affected by the proposed resolution; and

      (iv) where the proposed resolution would designate private land, to the owner of that land or to the person assessed for the uniform business rate on it;

  (*c*) where subsection (4) below applies, they have obtained the necessary consent.

(4) This subsection applies—

  (*a*) where the resolution relates to a street which is owned or maintained by a relevant undertaker; and (*b*) where the resolution designates as a licence street any street maintained by a highway authority;

and in subsection (3) above "necessary consent" means—

(i) in the case mentioned in paragraph (*a*) above, the consent of the relevant undertaker; and

(ii) in the case mentioned in paragraph (*b*) above, the consent of the highway authority.

(5) The following are relevant undertakers for the purposes of this section:—

(*a*) Railtrack PLC; and

(*b*) the British Waterways Board.

(6) The notice referred to in subsection (3) above shall—

(*a*) contain a draft of the resolution to which it relates; and

(*b*) state that representations or a request to hear representations relating to it may be made in writing to the council within such period, not less than 28 days after the publication of the notice, as may be specified in the notice.

(7) As soon as practicable after the expiry of the period specified under subsection (6) above, the council shall consider any written representations relating to the proposed resolution which they have received before the expiry of that period or, if requested to hear oral representations, shall hear the representations at a place and time notified to the person making the request.

(8) After the council have considered those representations, they may if they think fit, pass the proposed resolution with any modifications they consider appropriate as a result of any representations under this section.

(9) As soon as practicable after passing a resolution under subsection (8) above the council shall by notice in writing inform all persons given notice of the proposed resolution.

(10) The council shall publish notice of the passing of such a resolution in a local newspaper circulating in their area on two consecutive weeks.

(11) The first publication shall not be later than 28 days before the day specified in the resolution for the coming into force of the designation.

PART VI

MISCELLANEOUS

45.—(1) The provisions of Part VII of the Act of 1939 (which makes provision in relation to dangerous and neglected structures) shall apply to outer London boroughs.

(2) Section 43 of the London Government Act 1963 (which provides for modifications to the extent of the application of the London Building Acts) is amended by the insertion, in subsection (1), after the words "Part II" in both places where they appear, of the words "and Part VII".

Dangerous structures.

1963 c. 33.

1994 c. xii.

(3) The council of an outer London borough to which Part VII of the said Act of 1939 is applied under this section may make regulations under section 8 (Dangerous structure fees) of the London Local Authorities Act 1994 as though they were a borough to which the London Building Acts apply.

1984 c. 55.

(4) Section 77 of the Building Act 1984 (which makes provision in relation to dangerous buildings) and section 79 of that Act (which makes provision in relation to ruinous and dilapidated buildings and neglected sites) shall not apply to an outer London borough.

(5) Paragraph 5 of Schedule 3 to the said Act of 1984 shall apply in respect of the borough of a participating council as though "77 to 83" were replaced by "77 to 80, 82, 83".

(6) In this section—

"outer London borough" has the same meaning as in section 1(1) of the said Act of 1963 but does not include the London Borough of Barnet;

1939 c. xcvii.

"the Act of 1939" means the London Building Acts (Amendment) Act 1939; and

1952 c. viii.
1954 c. xxiv.

"the London Building Acts" means the London Building Acts 1930 to 1939 as amended by the London County Council (General Powers) Act 1952 and by the London County Council (General Powers) Act 1954.

Service of certain notices under Highways Act 1980.
1980 c. 66.

46.—(1) Where a participating council issues a notice under section 149(1) (Removal of things so deposited on highways so as to be a nuisance etc.) of the Highways Act 1980 and the name or the address of the person who deposited the thing on the highway to which the notice relates cannot after reasonable enquiry be ascertained by the council seeking to serve the notice, the notice may be served by—

(*a*) addressing it to the person on whom it is to be served by the description of "owner" of the thing (describing it) to which the notice relates; and

(*b*) affixing it or a copy of it to the thing.

(2) The provisions of this section are without prejudice to the provisions of section 322 (Service of notices etc.) of the said Act of 1980.

Compensation to servants of fire authority.
1921 c. l.

47. Section 31 (Compensation to persons in Council's service on abolition of office) of the London County Council (General Powers) Act 1921 shall (with any necessary modifications) apply to the London Fire and Civil Defence Authority as it applies in relation to a London borough council.

Bus lanes.

1996 c. ix.

48. Section 4 (Penalty charge notices under Part II) of and Schedule 1 (which makes provision relating to the enforcement of the provisions relating to bus lanes) to the London Local Authorities Act 1996 are amended in accordance with Schedule 2 to this Act.

Fees for assistance given in relation to entertainment licensed by the Crown.

49. Where a participating council is requested to consider, approve or carry out safety measures, crowd control measures or related matters in relation to premises used for any entertainment lawfully held by licence of the Crown, the council may charge a fee to cover in whole or in part the reasonable administrative or other costs of considering, approving or carrying out those measures.

50.—(1) Any person who—

    (*a*) intentionally obstructs any authorised officer acting in the exercise of his powers under this Act; or

    (*b*) without reasonable cause fails to give any authorised officer any assistance or information which the officer may reasonably require of him for the purposes of the exercise of the officer's functions under any provision of this Act;

shall be guilty of an offence and liable on summary conviction to a fine not exceeding level 3 on the standard scale.

(2) Subsection (1)(*b*) above applies in relation to a constable as it applies in relation to an authorised officer.

(3) A person shall be guilty of an offence if, in giving any information which is required of him by virtue of subsection (1)(*b*) above—

    (*a*) he makes any statement which he knows is false in a material particular; or

    (*b*) he recklessly makes a statement which is false in a material particular.

(4) A person guilty of an offence under subsection (3) above shall be liable on summary conviction to a fine not exceeding level 5 on the standard scale.

51.—(1) In proceedings for an offence under this Act it shall be a defence for the person charged to prove that he took all reasonable precautions and exercised all due diligence to avoid the commission of the offence.

(2) If in any case the defence provided under subsection (1) above involves the allegation that the commission of the offence was due to the act or default of another person, the person charged shall not, without leave of the court, be entitled to rely on that defence unless, no later than 7 clear days before the hearing, he has served on the prosecutor a notice in writing giving such information as was then in his possession identifying or assisting in the identification of that other person.

52.—(1) Where an offence under this Act committed by a body corporate is proved to have been committed with the consent or connivance of, or to be attributable to any neglect on the part of, a director, manager, secretary or other similar officer of the body corporate or any person who was purporting to act in any such capacity, he, as well as the body corporate, shall be guilty of the offence.

(2) Where the affairs of the body corporate are managed by its members, subsection (1) above shall apply to the acts and defaults of a member in connection with his functions of management as if he were a director of the body corporate.

SCHEDULES

SCHEDULE 1

LONDON GOVERNMENT ACT 1963 SCHEDULE 12 AS HAVING EFFECT IN
ACCORDANCE WITH PART IV (LICENSING) OF THIS ACT

SCHEDULE 12

LICENSING OF PUBLIC ENTERTAINMENTS IN GREATER LONDON ON AND
AFTER 1ST APRIL 1965

Music and dancing licences

1.—(1) *** No premises in a London borough or the City of London, whether or not licensed for the sale of intoxicating liquor, shall be used for any of the following purposes, that is to say, public dancing or music and any other public entertainment of the like kind, except under and in accordance with the terms of a licence granted under this paragraph by the council of that borough or the Common Council, as the case may be, and that council or the Common Council is in this Schedule referred to as "the Council".

(2) The Council may grant to *** an applicant and from time to time renew or transfer a licence for the use of any premises specified therein for all or any of the purposes aforesaid on such terms and conditions and subject to such restrictions as may be so specified.

(3) Subject to the next following sub-paragraph and to paragraph 19(3) of this Schedule, a licence granted under this paragraph shall, unless previously cancelled under paragraph 8 or revoked under paragraph 9A or 10(4) or (4A) of this Schedule, remain in force for one year or for such shorter period specified in the licence as the Council may think fit.

(4) The Council may grant a licence under this paragraph in respect of such one or more particular occasions only as may be specified in the licence, and a licence granted by virtue of this sub-paragraph is hereafter in this Schedule referred to as an "occasional licence".

* * * * *

(6) Sub-paragraph (1) of this paragraph shall not apply to any entertainment lawfully held by virtue of letters patent or licence of the Crown.

(7) In this paragraph "premises" includes any place.

2.—(1) An applicant for the grant, renewal or transfer of a licence under paragraph 1 or the variation of such a licence under paragraph 18 of this Schedule shall, not later than the day the application is made, send a copy of the application to the commissioner of police in whose area the premises are situated (in this Schedule referred to as "the commissioner") and to the London Fire and Civil Defence Authority (in this Schedule referred to as "the fire authority") and, subject to sub-paragraph (2) below, no such application shall be considered by the Council unless the applicant complies with this sub-paragraph.

(2) Where an application for the grant, renewal, transfer or variation of a licence has been made and the applicant has failed to send a copy of the application in accordance with the requirement of sub-paragraph (1) above the Council may, in such cases as they think fit and after duly consulting with the party who was not supplied with a copy of the said application, waive such a requirement.

(3) In considering any such application the Council shall have regard to any observations submitted to them by the commissioner and the fire authority within twenty-eight days of the making of the application and may have regard to any observation submitted by them thereafter.

(4) An applicant for any such grant, renewal, transfer or variation of a licence shall furnish such particulars and give such other notices, including the public advertisement of the application, as the Council may by regulation prescribe.

(5) Save where a shorter period is agreed by the Council, an applicant for the grant of an occasional licence shall make such application not less than twenty-eight days in advance of the occasion for which the occasional licence is sought and shall send a copy of the application to the Commissioner and to the fire authority.

(6) Regulations under sub-paragraph (4) above may prescribe the procedure for determining applications.

2A.—(1) This paragraph applies where the Council by whom a licence was granted under paragraph 1 of this Schedule in respect of any premises receive a report from the commissioner of police in whose district the premises are situated—

(*a*) stating that there is a serious problem relating to the supply or use of controlled drugs at the premises or at any premises nearby which are controlled by the holder of the licence; and

(*b*) giving reasons for his view that there is such a problem.

(2) An application for the renewal or transfer of the licence may be refused by the Council on the ground that they are satisfied that not renewing or transferring it will significantly assist in dealing with the problem.

(3) The Council shall give the reasons for their refusal of the application to—

(*a*) the holder of the licence; and

(*b*) in the case of an application for the transfer of the licence, the person to whom the licence would have been transferred if the application had been granted.

(4) A person to whom reasons are given may make representations to the Council; and the Council shall consider any representations within the period of twenty-one days beginning with the day on which they receive them.

(5) After considering any representations, the Council shall (unless the date of expiry of the licence has passed) either—

(*a*) confirm the refusal of the application; or

(*b*) grant the application.

(6) The Council shall have regard in exercising their functions under this paragraph to such guidance as may be issued by the Secretary of State.

(7) In this paragraph "premises" includes any place.

3. The person making an application for the grant, renewal or transfer of a licence under paragraph 1 of this Schedule (except where the licence is for an entertainment which in the opinion of the Council is of an educational or other like character or is given for a charitable or other like purpose) on making the application pay to the Council such fee as the Council may fix.

Indoor sports licences

3A.—(1) Subject to sub-paragraphs (2) and (3) below, no premises in a London borough or the City of London shall be used for any entertainment which consists of any sporting event to which the public are invited as spectators (a "sports entertainment") except under and in accordance with the terms of a licence granted under this paragraph by the Council.

(2) Sub-paragraph (1) above does not require a licence in respect of any occasion when the sporting event which constitutes the entertainment is not the principal purpose for which the premises are used on that occasion; but this provision does not apply in relation to a sports complex.

(3) Sub-paragraph (1) above does not apply to a sports entertainment held in a pleasure fair.

(4) The Council may grant to *** an applicant, and from time to time renew or transfer, a licence for the use of any premises specified in it for any sports entertainment on such terms and conditions and subject to such restrictions as may be so specified.

(5) Subject to the next following sub-paragraph and to paragraph 19(3) of this Schedule, a licence granted under this paragraph shall, unless previously cancelled under paragraph 8 or revoked under paragraph 10(4) of this Schedule, remain in force for one year or for such shorter period specified in the licence as the Council think fit.

(6) the Council may grant a licence under this paragraph in respect of such one or more particular occasions only as may be specified in the licence, and a licence granted by virtue of this sub-paragraph is hereafter in this Schedule referred to as an "occasional sports licence".

* * * * *

(8) In this paragraph—

"premises" means any permanent or temporary building and any tent or inflatable structure and includes a part of a building where the building is a sports complex but does not include a part of any other building;

"sporting event" means any contest, exhibition or display of any sport;

"sports complex" means a building—

(*a*) which provides accommodation and facilities for both those engaging in sport and spectators; and (*b*) the parts of which are so arranged that one or more sports can be engaged in simultaneously in different parts of the building; and

"sport" includes any game in which physical skill is the predominant factor and any form of physical recreation which is also engaged in for purposes of competition or display, except dancing (in any form).

3B.—(1) An applicant for the grant, renewal or transfer of a licence under paragraph 3A or the variation of such a licence under paragraph 18 of this Schedule shall, not later than the day the application is made, send a copy of the application to the commissioner and to the fire authority and, subject to sub-paragraph (2) below, no such application shall be considered by the Council unless the applicant complies with this sub-paragraph.

(2) Where an application for the grant, renewal, transfer or variation of a licence has been made and the applicant has failed to send a copy of the application in accordance with the requirement of sub-paragraph (1) above the Council may, in such cases as they think fit and after duly consulting with the party who was not supplied with a copy of the said application, waive such a requirement.

(3) In considering any such application the Council shall have regard to any observations submitted to them by the commissioner and the fire authority within twenty-eight days of the making of the application and may have regard to any observation submitted by them thereafter.

(4) An applicant for any such grant, renewal, transfer or variation of a licence shall furnish such particulars and give such other notices, including the public advertisement of the application, as the Council may by regulation prescribe.

(5) Regulations under sub-paragraph (4) above may prescribe the procedure for determining applications.

3C. The person making an application for the grant, renewal or transfer of a licence under paragraph 3A of this Schedule shall on making the application pay to the Council such fee as the Council may fix.

Boxing and wrestling licences

4.—(1) This paragraph shall apply to any boxing or wrestling entertainment (that is to say, any public contest, exhibition or display of boxing or, as the case may be, wrestling) which is provided wholly or mainly in the open air in Greater London other than such an entertainment provided—

(*a*) by a travelling showman at a pleasure fair;

(*b*) by members of the Boy Scouts' Association or of any organisation constituted by the Boy Scouts' Association in pursuance of their charter;

(*c*) by any school; or

(*d*) by a bona fide association, club, hospital or society not carried on for profit.

(2) A boxing or wrestling entertainment to which this paragraph applies shall not be given elsewhere than at premises licensed for the purpose in accordance with the provisions of this paragraph and in accordance with the terms of that licence.

(3) The Council may grant to *** an applicant and from time to time renew or transfer a licence to use any premises specified therein for the purpose of a boxing or wrestling entertainment on such terms and conditions and subject to such restrictions as may be so specified.

(4) Subject to the next following sub-paragraph and to paragraph 19(3) of this Schedule, a licence granted under this paragraph shall, unless previously cancelled under paragraph 8 or revoked under paragraph 10(4) of this Schedule, remain in force for one year or for such shorter period specified in the licence as the Council may think fit.

(5) The Council may grant a licence under this paragraph in respect of such one or more particular occasions only as may be specified in the licence, and a licence granted by virtue of this sub-paragraph is hereafter in this Schedule referred to as an "occasional outdoor boxing or wrestling licence".

* * * * *

(7) In this paragraph "premises" includes any place.

5.—(1) An applicant for the grant, renewal, transfer or variation of a licence under paragraph 4 or the variation of such a licence under paragraph 18 of this Schedule shall not later than the day the application is made send a copy of the application to the Commissioner and to the fire authority and, subject to sub-paragraph (2) below, no such application shall be considered by the Council unless the applicant complies with this sub-paragraph.

(2) Where an application for the grant, renewal, transfer or variation of a licence has been made and the applicant has failed to send a copy of the application in accordance with the requirement of sub-paragraph (1) above the Council may, in such cases as they think fit and after duly consulting with the party who was not supplied with a copy of the said application, waive such a requirement.

(3) In considering any such application the Council shall have regard to any observations submitted to them by the Commissioner and the fire authority within twenty-eight days of the making of the application and may have regard to any observation submitted by them thereafter.

(4) An applicant for any such grant, renewal, transfer or variation of a licence shall furnish such particulars and give such other notices, including the public advertisement of the application, as the Council may by regulation prescribe.

(5) Regulations under sub-paragraph (4) above may prescribe the procedure for determining applications.

6. The person making an application for the grant, renewal or transfer of a licence under paragraph 4 of this Schedule shall on making the application pay to the Council such fee as the Council may fix.

6A. Subject to paragraph 6C of this Schedule, where, before the date of expiry of a licence granted under paragraph 1, 3A or 4 of this Schedule, an application has been made for the renewal of that licence, the licence shall be deemed to remain in force, notwithstanding that the date of expiry of the licence has passed, until the determination of the application by the Council or until the withdrawal of the application.

6B. Subject to paragraph 6C of this Schedule, where, before the date of expiry of a licence granted under paragraph 1, 3A or 4 of this Schedule, an application has been made for the transfer of that licence, the licence shall be deemed to remain in force (with any necessary modifications) notwithstanding that the date of expiry of the licence has passed, or that the applicant for such transfer is carrying on at the premises in respect of which the licence was granted the functions to which the licence relates, until the determination of the application by the Council or the withdrawal of the application.

6C.—(1) The following provisions of this paragraph shall have effect as respects cases where, before the date of expiry of a licence granted under paragraph 1, 3A or 4 of this Schedule an application for renewal of the licence has been made ("a renewal case") or an application for transfer of the licence has been made ("a transfer case").

(2) If the application is not determined before the prospective expiry date, the licence shall not be deemed to remain in force under paragraph 6A or 6B of this Schedule, as the case may be, after that date and the application shall be deemed to be withdrawn on that date, unless before then the applicant pays the Council a continuation fee.

(3) Where a continuation fee is paid in pursuance of sub-paragraph (2) of this paragraph in a renewal case, the applicant's application for renewal shall be deemed to be an application for renewal for a period of twelve months starting on the day following the prospective expiry date.

(4) Where a continuation fee is paid in pursuance of sub-paragraph (2) of this paragraph in a transfer case—

(*a*) the applicant shall be deemed to have made an application for the renewal of the licence for a period of twelve months starting on the day following the prospective expiry date;

(*b*) the Council shall determine the application for transfer and deemed application for renewal together; and

(*c*) in the following provisions of this paragraph, references to "the application" in a transfer case are references to the application for transfer and the application for renewal.

(5) If the application is not determined before the date of the expiry of the renewal period under sub-paragraph (3) or (4) of this paragraph, as the case may be, the licence shall not be deemed to remain in force under paragraph 6A or 6B of this Schedule, as the case may be, after that date, and the application shall be deemed to be withdrawn on that date, unless before then the applicant pays the Council a further continuation fee.

(6) Where a further continuation fee is paid in pursuance of sub-paragraph (5) of this paragraph, then—

(*a*) in a renewal case, the applicant's application for renewal shall be deemed to be an application for renewal for a period starting on the day following the date of the expiry of the renewal period under sub-paragraph (3) of this paragraph; and

(*b*) in a transfer case, the applicant's application so far as it is a deemed application for renewal shall be deemed to be an application for renewal for a period starting on the day following the date of the expiry of the renewal period under sub-paragraph (4) of this paragraph.

(7) A deemed application for renewal under paragraph (6) shall be for a period expiring—

(*a*) where the application is withdrawn, on the date of withdrawal;

(*b*) where the application is refused, on the date of the refusal;

(*c*) where the application is granted, on one or other of the following:—

(i) the date twelve months after the beginning of the period; or

(ii) such other date as may be specified by the Council when allowing the application.

(8) In this paragraph—

"the prospective expiry date" means—

(*a*) in a transfer case, the date on which the licence would have expired if the application for transfer had not been made; and

(*b*) in a renewal case, the date of the expiry of the period in respect of which the application for renewal of the licence was made;

"a continuation fee" is a fee of the same amount as the fee payable in respect of an application for renewal of a licence.

6D. Where an applicant for the transfer of a licence granted under paragraph 1, 3A or 4 of this Schedule is carrying on at the premises in respect of which the licence was granted the functions to which the licence relates, "any necessary modifications" where those words appear in paragraph 6B of this Schedule, means the substitution for the name of the licence holder of the name of the applicant for the transfer of the licence and any other necessary modifications.

Transmission and cancellation of licences

7. In the event of the death of the holder of a licence granted under paragraph 1, 3A or 4 of this Schedule, then, until a legal personal representative of the deceased holder has been duly constituted, the person carrying on at the premises in respect of which the licence was granted the functions to which the licence relates shall be deemed to be the holder of the licence unless and until it is transferred to some other person.

8. The Council upon receiving from the holder of a licence under paragraph 1, 3A or 4 of this Schedule which is for the time being in force a written request in that behalf accompanied by the licence may cancel the licence.

Power to impose general terms, conditions and restrictions by regulations

* * * * *

9.—(1) The Council may make regulations prescribing standard conditions applicable to all, or any class of, licences which may be granted under paragraph 1, 3A or 4 of this Schedule.

(2) Where the Council have made regulations under this paragraph, every licence granted, renewed or transferred by them shall be deemed to have been so granted, renewed or transferred subject to any standard conditions except so far as they are expressly excluded or amended in any particular case.

9A.—(1) This paragraph applies where the Council by whom a licence was granted under paragraph 1 of this Schedule in respect of any premises receive a report from the commissioner of police in whose district the premises are situated—

(*a*) stating that there is a serious problem relating to the supply or use of controlled drugs at the premises or at any premises nearby which are controlled by the holder of the licence; and

(*b*) giving reasons for his view that there is such a problem.

(2) The Council may—

(*a*) revoke the licence; or

(*b*) impose terms, conditions or restrictions on or subject to which it is to be held,

on the ground that they are satisfied that to do so will significantly assist in dealing with the problem.

(3) The Council shall give the reasons for their revocation of the licence, or the imposition of the terms, conditions or restrictions, to the holder of the licence who may make representations to the Council; and the Council shall consider any representations within the period of twenty-one days beginning with the day on which they receive them.

(4) After consideration of any representations, the Council shall (unless the date of expiry of the licence has passed) either—

(*a*) confirm that the licence remains revoked or continues to have effect on or subject to the terms, conditions or restrictions which have been imposed; or

(*b*) reinstate the licence or determine that it has effect free of those terms, conditions or restrictions.

(5) The Council shall have regard in exercising their functions under this paragraph to such guidance as may be issued by the Secretary of State.

(6) In this paragraph "premises" includes any place.

Enforcement of paragraphs 1 to 9

10.—(1) If at any premises any entertainment in respect of which a licence is required under paragraph 1, 3A or 4 of this Schedule is provided without such a licence being held in respect thereof, then—

(*a*) any person concerned in the organisation or management of that entertainment; and

(*b*) any other person who, knowing or having reasonable cause to suspect that such an entertainment would be so provided at those premises—

(i) allowed the premises to be used for the provision of that entertainment; or

(ii) let the premises, or otherwise made the premises available, to any person by whom an offence in connection with the entertainment has been committed,

shall be guilty of an offence.

(2) Subject to paragraph 11 of this Schedule, if—

(*a*) any person is the holder of a licence under the said paragraph 1, 3A or 4, under section 21 (Licensing of public exhibitions, etc.) of the Greater London Council (General Powers) Act 1966 or under section 5 (Licensing of entertainments booking offices) of the Greater London Council (General Powers) Act 1978 in respect of any premises which have been used in contravention of any term, condition or restriction on or subject to which the licence is held; or

1966 c. xxviii.

1978 c. xiii.

(*aa*) any person is an applicant for the transfer of a licence granted under paragraph 1, 3A or 4 of this Schedule where he is carrying on at the premises in respect of which the licence was granted the functions to which the licence relates in respect of any premises which have been used in contravention of any term, condition or restriction on or subject to which the licence is held; or

(*b*) any other person who, knowing or having reasonable cause to suspect that the premises would be so used—

(i) allowed the premises to be used; or

(ii) let the premises, or otherwise made the premises available, to any person who so used the premises;

he shall be guilty of an offence in respect of the contravention of each such term, condition or restriction.

(3) Any person guilty of an offence under sub-paragraph (1) or (2) of this paragraph shall be liable on summary conviction—

(*a*) in the case of an offence to which sub-paragraph (3A) of this paragraph applies, to a fine not exceeding £20,000 or to imprisonment for a term not exceeding six months or to both;

(*b*) in any other case, to a fine not exceeding level 5 on the standard scale or to imprisonment for a term not exceeding three months or to both.

(3A) This sub-paragraph applies to—

(*a*) any offence under sub-paragraph (1) of this paragraph where the entertainment provided is entertainment in respect of which a licence is required under paragraph (1) of this Schedule; and

(*b*) any offence under sub-paragraph (2) of this paragraph where the licence held is a licence granted under that paragraph and the term, condition or restriction which is contravened imposes a limit on the number of persons who may be present at the entertainment,

but excluding (in each case) any offence which would not be an offence if section 3 of the Greater London Council (General Powers) Act 1978 (premises used for public entertainment consisting wholly or partly of human posing deemed to be premises used for public dancing) had not been enacted.

(4) If the holder of a licence under the said paragraph 1, 3A or 4 is convicted by virtue of sub-paragraph (2)(*a*) of this paragraph, then, subject to paragraph 19 of this Schedule, the Council may revoke the licence.

(4A) Where a person is convicted by a court of an offence under sub-paragraph (2) of this paragraph in relation to a licence granted under paragraph 1 of this Schedule in respect of any premises, the court may revoke the licence if satisfied that—

(*a*) there is a serious problem relating to the supply or use of controlled drugs at the premises or at any premises nearby which are controlled by the holder of the licence; and

(*b*) it will significantly assist in dealing with the problem to revoke the licence.

SCH. 1
— *cont.*

(4B) The standard of proof for the purposes of sub-paragraph (4A) of this paragraph is that applicable in civil proceedings and in that sub-paragraph "premises" includes any place.

(5) Where an offence under sub-paragraph (1) or (2) of this paragraph committed by a body corporate is proved to have been committed with the consent or connivance of, or to be attributable to any neglect on the part of, any director, manager, secretary or other officer of the body corporate, or any person who was purporting to act in any such capacity, he as well as the body corporate shall be guilty of that offence and shall be liable to be proceeded against and punished accordingly.

(6) Where the affairs of a body corporate are managed by its members, sub-paragraph (5) above shall apply in relation to the acts and defaults of a member in connection with his functions of management as if he were a director of the body corporate.

11. Where, in the case of any premises in respect of which a licence under paragraph 1 of this Schedule is for the time being in force, a special order of exemption on any special occasion has been granted in respect of those premises under section 107 of the Licensing Act 1953, no person shall be guilty of an offence under paragraph 10(2) of this Schedule by reason only of those premises being kept open on that special occasion for any of the purposes authorised by the licence after the latest hour so authorised but not later than the hour specified in that special order as the hour for closing.

1953 c. 46.

12.—(1) A police constable or any person appointed for the purpose by the Council or the fire authority may at all reasonable times enter any premises in respect of which a licence under paragraph 1, 3A or 4 of this Schedule is for the time being in force at which he has reason to believe that an entertainment to which any of these paragraphs applies is being or is about to be given with a view to seeing whether the provisions of this Schedule applicable to that entertainment and the terms, conditions or restrictions on or subject to which the licence is held are complied with.

(2) A police constable or any person appointed as aforesaid may, if authorised in that behalf by a warrant granted by a justice of the peace, enter any premises in respect of which he has reason to suspect that an offence under this Schedule is being committed.

(3) Any person who refuses to permit any such constable or person to enter or inspect any premises in accordance with the provisions of this paragraph shall for every such refusal be liable on summary conviction to a fine not exceeding level 3 on the standard scale.

12A. The provisions of paragraphs 12B and 12C of this Schedule shall have effect in Greater London other than in the outer London boroughs.

12B.—(1) Subject to sub-paragraph (2) of this paragraph, the court by or before which a person is convicted of an offence under sub-paragraph (1) or (2) of paragraph 10 of this Schedule may order any thing produced to the court, and shown to the satisfaction of the court to relate to the offence, to be forfeited and dealt with in such manner as the court may order.

(2) The court shall not order any thing to be forfeited under the foregoing sub-paragraph where a person claiming to be the owner of or otherwise interested in it applies to be heard by the court, unless an opportunity has been given to him to show cause why the order should not be made.

12C. A constable or any person appointed for the purpose by the Council who enters any premises under the authority of a warrant granted under sub-paragraph (2) of paragraph 12 of this Schedule may seize and remove any apparatus or equipment or other thing whatsoever found on the premises which he has reasonable cause to believe may be liable to be forfeited under paragraph 12B of this Schedule.

Provisional grant of licences

17.—(1) Where application is made to the Council for the grant of a licence under paragraph 1, 3A or 4 of this Schedule in respect of premises which are to be, or are in the course of being, constructed, extended or altered and the Council are satisfied that the premises would, if completed *** in accordance with the requirements of the Council, be such that the Council would grant the licence, the Council may grant the licence subject to a condition that it shall be of no effect until confirmed by the Council.

(2) The Council shall, on an application being made for the appropriate variation of the licence, confirm any licence granted by virtue of the foregoing sub-paragraph if and when they are satisfied that the premises have been completed in accordance with the *** requirements aforesaid, or in accordance with those *** requirements as modified by the Council, and that the licence is held by a fit and proper person.

Variation of licences

18. The holder of a licence in respect of any premises granted under paragraph 1, 3A or 4 of this Schedule may at any time apply to the Council for such variations of the terms, conditions or restrictions on or subject to which the licence is held as may be specified in the application; and, subject to paragraph 19 of this Schedule, on any such application the Council may make such variations in any of those terms, conditions or restrictions, whether or not those specified in the application, as they think appropriate or may refuse the application.

18A. The person making an application for the variation of a licence under paragraph 18 of this Schedule shall on making the application pay to the Council such reasonable fee as the Council may fix.

Appeals

19.—(1) Any of the following persons, that is to say—

(*a*) an applicant for—

(i) the grant, renewal or transfer of a licence in respect of any premises under paragraph 1, 3A or 4 of this Schedule; or

(iii) the variation of the terms, conditions or restrictions on or subject to which any such licence as aforesaid is held,

whose application is refused;

(*b*) the holder of any such licence as aforesaid whose licence is revoked by the Council or who is aggrieved by any term, condition or restriction on or subject to which the licence is held,

may at any time before the expiration of the relevant period, appeal to a magistrates' court acting for the petty sessions area in which the premises are situated; and the court may make such order as it thinks fit and, subject to sub-paragraph (2) of this paragraph, that order shall be binding on the Council.

(1A) In this paragraph "relevant period" means the period of twenty-one days beginning with the date when the person in question is notified of—

　　(*a*) the refusal of his application;

　　(*b*) the revocation of his licence; or

　　(*c*) the imposition of the term, condition or restriction by which he is aggrieved;

but in a case where a decision is made under paragraph 2A(5) or 9A(4) of this Schedule means the date on which the person in question is notified of the decision.

(2) Any person aggrieved by the order of a magistrates' court under sub-paragraph (1) of this paragraph or under paragraph 10(4A) of this Schedule may appeal therefrom to the Crown Court.

(3) Subject to paragraph 19AA of this Schedule, where any such licence as aforesaid is revoked under paragraph 10(4) of this Schedule or an application for the renewal of a licence under the said paragraph 1, 3A or 4 is refused, otherwise than on the ground specified in paragraph 2A(2) of this Schedule, the licence shall be deemed to remain in force—

　　(*a*) during any period within which an appeal under this paragraph may be brought and, if such an appeal is brought within the relevant period, until the determination or abandonment of the appeal; and

　　(*b*) where such an appeal relating to such a refusal as aforesaid is successful and no further such appeal is available, until the licence is renewed by the Council.

(3A) A court which revokes a licence under paragraph 10(4A) of this Schedule may, if in the particular circumstances it would be unfair not to do so, order that the licence shall remain in force—

　　(*a*) during the period within which an appeal against the revocation may be brought; and

　　(*b*) if such an appeal is duly brought, until the determination or abandonment of the appeal.

(4) In the case of an appeal in relation to an application of which, in accordance with paragraph 2(1), 3B(1) or 5(1) of this Schedule, notice was required to be given to a commissioner of police, notice of that appeal shall be given to that commissioner as well as to any other person to whom it is required to be given apart from this sub-paragraph.

(5) Where any licence is renewed under paragraph 1, 3A or 4 of this Schedule and the Council specify any term, condition or restriction which was not previously specified in relation to that licence, the licence shall be deemed to be free of it until the time for bringing an appeal under this paragraph has expired and, if such an appeal is duly brought, until the determination or abandonment of the appeal.

19AA.—(1) The following provisions of this paragraph shall have effect as respects cases where an appeal under paragraph 19 of this Schedule is brought, within the period for doing so, against the revocation of a licence ("a revocation case") or against the refusal of an application for renewal of a licence ("a refusal case").

(2) If the appeal is not determined before the prospective expiry date, the licence shall not be deemed to remain in force under paragraph 19(3) of this Schedule after that date, and the appeal shall be deemed to be abandoned on that date, unless before then—

(*a*) in a revocation case, the appellant makes an application for the renewal of the licence for a period of twelve months starting on the day following the prospective expiry date;

(*b*) in a refusal case the appellant pays the council a continuation fee.

(3) Where a continuation fee is paid in pursuance of sub-paragraph (2)(*b*) of this paragraph, the appellant's refused application for renewal shall be deemed to be an application for renewal for a period of twelve months starting on the day following the prospective expiry date.

(4) If the appeal is not determined before the date of the expiry of the renewal period under sub-paragraph (2)(*a*) or (3) of this paragraph, as the case may be, the licence shall not be deemed to remain in force under paragraph 19(3) of this Schedule after that date, and the appeal shall be deemed to be abandoned on that date, unless before then the appellant pays the council a continuation fee or, as the case may be, a further continuation fee.

(5) Where a continuation fee or a further continuation fee is paid in pursuance of sub-paragraph (4) of this paragraph, the appellant's application for renewal or, as the case may be, refused application for renewal shall be deemed to be an application for renewal for a period starting on the day following the date of the expiry of the renewal period under sub-paragraph (2)(*a*) or, as the case may be, sub-paragraph (3) of this paragraph.

(6) A deemed application for renewal under sub-paragraph (5) shall be for a period expiring—

(*a*) where the appeal is withdrawn, on the date of withdrawal;

(*b*) where the appeal is unsuccessful—

(i) if a further appeal is available but is not made within the period for doing so, on the date of the expiry of that period;

(ii) if no further appeal is available, on the date of the decision of the court;

(*c*) where the appeal is successful, on the day before the date of the next anniversary of the beginning of the period; provided that where the period, at the time of the decision of the court, has been running for more than twelve months, the court may specify an earlier date.

(7) In this paragraph—

"the prospective expiry date" means—

(*a*) in a revocation case, the date on which the licence would have expired if it had not been revoked; and

(*b*) in a refusal case, the date of the expiry of the period in respect of which the refused application for renewal of the licence was made;

"a continuation fee" is a fee of the same amount as the fee payable in respect of an application for renewal of a licence.

Interpretation

19A. In this Schedule "controlled drugs" has the same meaning as in the Misuse of Drugs Act 1971.

SCHEDULE 2

AMENDMENTS TO SECTION 4 (PENALTY CHARGE NOTICES UNDER PART II) OF Section 48.
AND SCHEDULE 1 (ENFORCEMENT NOTICES, ETC., UNDER PART II (BUS LANES) 1996 c. ix.
OF THIS ACT) TO THE LONDON LOCAL AUTHORITIES ACT 1996

1. In subsection (2) of section 4, after "with respect to a vehicle" the words ", by the owner of the vehicle," are inserted.

2. In paragraph 1 of Schedule 1—

   (*a*) in sub-paragraph (1)(*a*) the words "or paragraph 4(1) below" are left out;

   (*b*) at the end of sub-paragraph (*b*) the word "and" is left out;

   (*c*) sub-paragraph (1)(*c*) is left out;

   (*d*) at the end of sub-paragraph (i) the word "or" is left out;

   (*e*) paragraph (ii) is left out.

3. In paragraph 2 of Schedule 1—

   (*a*) in the heading the words "penalty charge notice or" are left out;

   (*b*) in sub-paragraph (1) the words "a penalty charge notice has been served under section 4 (Penalty charge notices under Part II) of this Act, or paragraph 4(1) below or a person on whom" are left out;

   (*c*) in sub-paragraph (3) the words "penalty charge notice or" are left out;

   (*d*) in sub-paragraph (4)(*a*) the words from the beginning to "enforcement notice was served" are left out;

   (*e*) after sub-paragraph (4)(*b*) insert "; or";

   (*f*) the following sub-paragraph is substituted for sub-paragraph (4)(*c*)— "(*c*) that at the time the alleged breach of such order or regulations took place the person who was in control of the vehicle was in control of the vehicle without the consent of the owner.";

   (*g*) sub-paragraphs (7), (8) and (9) are left out.

4. In sub-paragraphs 3(1)(*a*) and 3(1)(*b*) of Schedule 1 the words "penalty charge notice or" are left out.

5. In sub-paragraph 3(2) of Schedule 1 the words "a penalty charge notice or" where they appear the first time are replaced by the word "an".

6. Paragraph 4 of Schedule 1 is left out.

7. In paragraph 8 of Schedule 1—

   (*a*) in sub-paragraph (1) the words "a penalty charge notice or" are replaced by the word "an";

   (*b*) sub-paragraph (2) is left out.

8. In paragraph 11 of Schedule 1 the words "a penalty charge notice or" are replaced by the word "an".

Printed in the UK for The Stationery Office Limited under the authority and superintendence of Carol Tullo, Controller of Her Majesty's Stationery Office and Queen's Printer of Acts of Parliament